# The Real Hawaii Life

## True Stories of Relocations to Hawaii

# KAT VARANO

The Real Hawaii Life

For information about this title or to order other books and/or electronic media, contact the publisher:

Walk By Faith Publishing, LLC
P.O. Box 69943
Tucson, AZ 85737

We welcome any comments, questions or contributions you may have for future editions. Please send to the address above or inquire through The Real Hawaii Life's website at www.therealhawaiilife.com.

ISBN: 978-0-692-42183-3

Print in the United States of America

# TABLE OF CONTENTS

# FOREWORD

Author Kat Varano toyed with the idea of relocating to the Islands, but first she wanted to find out exactly what that would entail. Hence, the idea of connecting with *real* people who had made the move was hatched.

Varano interviewed a wide variety of individuals from *20-somethings* to *the solidly retired.* She asked them the same questions and wove their answers into a tapestry of intriguing real-life stories, or case files, that comprise the chapters of her book.

As a result, you'll get to know those interviewed by their first names. You'll delve into their finances and learn how they shipped their pets, cars, furniture, clothes, and various other items they couldn't leave behind. You'll see how they had to modify their grocery lists and housing expectations to fit the often astonishing *island cost* of food and lodging. You'll follow them as they search for employment, make decisions on where to send their children to school, research the *flavors* of different neighborhoods, develop ways to socialize with others, and adapt to the *island lifestyle.* Also helpful are lists of *likes, dislikes, regrets,* and *best advice* as well as useful websites and other resources.

Varano's book *The Real Hawaii Life: True Stories of Relocations to Hawaii* is an enjoyable, interesting read and a valuable tool if you're contemplating a move to the Hawaiian Islands.

**"Thinking about moving to Hawaii?
DON'T . . . until you read this book."**

Mary Ann Pierotti

# CONFESSION

I must confess. Like you, I have often contemplated relocating to Hawaii from the *mainland* (the continental United States) especially following one of my numerous visits to the islands. The thought of moving to Hawaii kept lingering—affected by the extreme summer weather in the Sonoran desert, otherwise known as my hometown (aka Southern Arizona). Here, we're reluctant to exit a building unless running at top speed to get out of the heat and always needing sunscreen, a hat, and sunglasses. This alone is motivation to pick up and seek a locale with a moderate temperature.

But my thoughts of moving to Hawaii have continually and apprehensively been squashed when the reality was transcribed from pen to paper. The guarantee of subsistence on a remote island was at best questionable. Regardless of my dozen visits to the islands and countless hours of research, I needed to know more.

## My Fact-finding Journey

The antidote to abandoning the idea of living in Hawaii was research. So I visited blog after blog about Hawaii to get the extra bits of key information I needed to finally ignite a move to the islands. My Hawaii fact-finding journey carried me through bookstores where I scoured the shelves for travelogues, how-to books, relocation guides—anything to help cement my plans. Plus I must have visited every Hawaii real estate website seeking the *one line* that would give me confidence to take the leap and move to paradise.

Watching home-buying television shows didn't give me answers, either. But I still recorded every episode—the new ones and the repeats—to make sure I didn't miss any gem of information! I came to realize the lucky ones on those shows made up a tiny percentage of people who saved money and planned well enough into their middle-age to afford relocating. This realization spurred me to do yet more research.

Mostly, I found facts about restaurants, beaches, and weather. They were useful for a one- or two-week vacation to Hawaii, but nothing about the feasibility of a relocation. What about the discrimination I'd heard so much about? Which cities and neighborhoods should I avoid? What is the reality of a newcomer getting a job? What about the schools for my young child—are they good or bad? I needed to hear the truth, and I couldn't find it.

So I did even more research—enough to conclude what I desperately missed in my portfolio was simply not available. I yearned to talk to people who had moved to paradise. What were *their* unabridged relocation stories?

I expect you purchased this book for the same reason I wrote it—because of a lack of resources describing real-life, in-depth accounts of relocation experiences to Hawaii. I had the silly notion (backed by research) that no book like this existed. So as Toni Morrison, a Pulitzer and Nobel Prize winner and *New York Times* bestselling author, astutely said, "If there's a book you really want to read, but it hasn't been written yet, then you must write it." I had to face facts: The questions I needed answered had to be answered by me.

### "Then It Hit Me!"

I had some writing experience while working toward a journalism degree in college. Between classes, I wrote feature articles for the school newspaper, interviewing interesting people and formulating messy notes into relevant articles.

Then it hit me. *Why don't I interview people who have relocated to Hawaii?*

Saying yes to this idea catapulted more research and fed my desire to write *The REAL Hawaii Life*. In the process, every single person who agreed to be interviewed asked me *why* I was writing this book. At first, I said I was curious, which was true. From there, it escalated to being on a mission for the truth. Then it evolved into deciding if I really wanted to relocate to Hawaii.

Now that I've finished 30 interviews and included 22 of them in this book, I can say for certain all of these reasons are true.

How did I recruit the people I interviewed? In a variety of ways. Some I knew personally, and some I found through obscure means (I will not tell!). The common thread was this: They also wished they'd had detailed, personal information before they relocated. That kind of insight would have saved them a lot of time, effort, money, and heartache!

Many people you'll meet through these 22 case files poured their hearts out as they shared their triumphs and failures. You may connect with some based on shared personality, goals, and tolerances. You may root for some to keep their dreams alive. And you may hope that others go back to the mainland. One thing is sure: when you finish reading this book, you'll be able to make your own decision about relocating to Hawaii.

## "Do I Still Plan to Move to Paradise?"

What about me? Do I still plan to move to paradise? You'll find out in the second edition of this book. And also look for updates to some of the stories you'll read about here.

I hope you enjoy *The REAL Hawaii Life* and find the depth of information you're seeking!

Hawaii

# BRIEFING ON THE CASE FILES

Welcome to the first book dedicated to the dreams and real-life experiences of the interviewees who moved to Hawaii!

The case files in this book feature experiences before, during, and after their relocations to five of the Hawaiian Islands: Oahu, Kauai, Maui, the Big Island, and Molokai. The people interviewed (I call them participants) did so willingly at length on the telephone, via email, and in person. Their stories are their true experiences.

This book is informational only, presented in the form of cases. My own opinions are omitted. As objectively as I could, I relayed facts from the participants' perspective, giving each story to you the way it was given to me—authentic and uncensored. It does not claim to be an account of facts and events but rather it reflects personal experiences in a factual way. Every attempt was made to clarify facts stated by the participants. Most of the stories contain their real names; those that do not are noted with an asterisk (*) beside the participant's name.

Throughout the interview process, many participants would change their minds, wouldn't complete the interview or clarify key information, or would refuse to sign the release and authorization to publish their stories. Some participants even wanted information taken out of the final publication. This book is *true* and I mean *true!* I wasn't willing to fabricate anyone's experiences to make that person *sound or look better*. Instead, either I didn't publish his or her story, or I changed names and other identifying features and removed photos.

Although I assure you these case files portray the participants' actual experiences, I purposely left out information I thought could be harmful to them and/or their families. This included children's names, serious health issues, and extremely negative remarks about companies and people.

I also did not judge whether the participants' experiences happened the way they described them, knowing that every event is based on perspectives from one's own cultural experiences. Rather, I did my best to leave them intact but omitted the names of companies or persons when necessary.

The key that follows will help you understand the book's structure and format.

## Structure of Cases

**Interviews:** Most of the interviews were conducted on the phone with only one person, regardless if that individual relocated with a spouse, family, or significant other. Therefore, because of this you may see that some interviews are entirely one-sided. Generally, a couple or a family will have had the same experience but with sometimes differing perspectives on it. In the end, I deemed each case as described to be an accurate account. It was also my experience that when speaking with a male in the family, information was not as forthcoming as I preferred. This is why many of the interviewees are female.

**Headings:** Each heading consists of a person's or persons' name, children or pets, age, total time living in Hawaii, and the island of relocation.

**Perpetrator(s):** The first person listed is the person who was interviewed. His or her age at the time of the interview (not the age when he or she relocated) is noted inside the parenthesis. The adult person who relocated *with* him or her (if applicable) or has played a major role in the participant's relocation experience is listed as a perpetrator as well.

**Accomplice(s):** This refers to the child(ren) and/or animal(s) that relocated *with* the participant(s), even if the participants have more children who live elsewhere. Exceptions to this rule occur if the persons have been married for a significant amount of time or if someone was pregnant.

**Time in Hawaii:** This time is calculated from when the participant landed on a Hawaiian island until the time the interview took place or the time the participant left Hawaii, whichever came first. A few of the participants who shared their stories have already returned to the mainland, which is noted within the stories if it was known at the time of writing. Note: .5 years equals six months (one-half year).

**Island:** This is the island where the participant relocated to most recently, regardless of the island he or she visited or lived on previously.

**Sections:** Each story features the same sections noted in bold print. However, not all sections contain the same information. That's because some participants were openly willing to share while others were very guarded. And plain and simple, some didn't have anything to share under certain sections. In case you're craving additional information, please be assured that *I did ask for it*. I wouldn't say I was intrusive, but I definitely expressed my desire to deliver information that was as complete as possible.

## What the Case Sections Include

Each story or case includes 16 sections, with the following kinds of information found in each section.

- **Background:** The participants' childhood and/or recent experiences that led to the relocation to Hawaii.

- **Finances:** How the participants funded and afforded a relocation.

- **Travel and Shipping:** The participants' shipping of personal belongings, vehicles, and pets, and getting around on the island.

- **Employment:** How participants found jobs, how the jobs were kept (or not!), how much the jobs paid, and tricks to getting hired.

- **Housing:** How participants found housing, tips to finding housing, descriptions of neighborhoods, and details of different areas on the islands.

- **Schooling:** What types of schooling were completed or attempted by participants, how much it cost, how long it took, and ins and outs of applying. Note: N/A means not applicable—that is, no school was attended on the islands.

- **Activities:** This includes participants' favorite (and not so favorite) activities from paddle boarding to snorkeling to hikes, what water and season is best for each activity, what dangers to watch out for, and what are good family and senior activities.

- **Socialization/Integration:** This conveys how participants integrated into the Hawaiian culture, tips to meeting people and getting connected in with others.

- **Helpful Resources:** Participants shared specific websites and names of companies that provided information or reasonably priced items, or people who provided good services.

- **Likes:** This lists the participants' favorites from hikes to beaches to restaurants to stores to areas of the island.

- **Dislikes:** This notes the participants' dislikes from restaurants to stores to neighborhoods to beaches to attitudes.

- **Best Moment:** This includes recollections of when participants' decision to move was solidified (or not) after arrival.

- **Regrets:** This notes things that would have been done differently in the moving process or survival skills the participants learned along the way.

- **Adaptation:** How and if the participants have adapted to island life.

- **Best Advice:** The participants' ideas about problems to avoid when relocating to Hawaii, how to make life easier when first arriving, and pitfalls to stay away from.

- **Verdict:** This notes whether or not the participants would stay in Hawaii.

## Keys to Using This Book

**Italicized Words:** When you see a word or a group of words in a row *italicized,* it is because the word or group of words is foreign to the English language. Sometimes, it is a small quote from the participant. Note: The foreign word will only be italicized the first time it appears in the book and will be accompanied by a definition. Thereafter, you can refer to the *Glossary* at the back of this book.

**Photos:** Some interview participants could not identify where their pictures were taken, so for those photos, no location is noted in the caption. The participants who did not want their names published do not have photos included with their stories.

**Authorization:** Most participants signed a consent form to release the information gathered during the interview process. If participants were unavailable (given the transient nature of the islands, this can happen) to sign the release or if they refused to sign it, then their actual names and pictures are not included.

**Conflicting Data:** Some participants provided information that may conflict with information in another story. Please understand that one's perspective can affect everything that's experienced! One person may think something is expensive while another person may think it's affordable. One person may think a hike is strenuous and another may think it's easy. Different perspectives depend upon different personalities, cultures, and experiences.

**Websites:** Every website that participants mentioned was verified to be active at the time of the interview.

**Glossary:** You'll find a *Glossary* in the back that includes definitions of foreign words and uncommon words used throughout.

Evans often kayaks in the
Hanalei and Wailua Rivers.

Evans enjoying the view in Waimea Canyon

# CASE #33201: LADIES FIRST

**Perpetrator(s):** Evans (31), Amy* (28)
**Accomplice(s):** None
**Time In Hawaii:** 4 Months
**Island:** Kauai

## BACKGROUND:

Traveling to Hawaii in high school may have instigated Evans's love of travel. His curiosity of other cultures turned him into a world explorer. He was fortunate to travel to at least a dozen remote, exotic locations all over the world including the Philippines, Thailand, Spain, Costa Rica, Ireland, and Belgium. He was even a Christian missionary in Kenya. Evans's volunteering later turned into becoming a pastor at a church. "I rarely return to the same destination," he shared, but that was all about to change.

While living in the frigid Michigan temperatures, Evans and his wife Amy were both eager to get to warm weather. Though he had traveled to many countries with warm weather, he discovered that, while living in Kenya, although he enjoyed interacting with

_____
* *Name Has Been Changed.*

other cultures, he had American roots. "The mid-upper class white American culture was my culture." It was then that Evans realized he wanted to explore warm-weather options within the United States.

Coupled with Evans's realization were his and Amy's different personalities. "She likes the beach. I like the mountains." Kauai seemed like a good match for both of them. The island was less developed and more remote than most of the United States, and it fit both of their senses of adventure.

Giving in to his usual plan of traveling to a new place, Evans purchased a round-trip ticket to Kauai, while a one-way ticket was purchased for Amy. Both then embarked on a complicated transition to Hawaii.

## FINANCES:

Evans and Amy were diligent in saving during their first five years of marriage. Prior to leaving for Kauai, they had about six months of living expenses saved in case neither one was able to secure employment on the island.

Evans and Amy dipped into their savings for about $1700 to purchase airline tickets to Kauai: a one-way ticket to Kauai for Amy; a round-trip ticket for Evans; and another one-way ticket for Evans. Amy's move to Kauai was permanent (as permanent as a move to Hawaii gets), Evans's round-trip ticket was to visit Amy two months later, and Evans's last one-way ticket was to move permanently. This would be about five months after Amy's initial move.

## TRAVEL AND SHIPPING:

Evans and Amy placed all of their belongings in a storage unit in Michigan prior to leaving the mainland, and they left their vehicle with a friend. They took the maximum allowable luggage on the airplane: three checked bags (the first bag was free). Evans made sure he took his inflatable kayak.

Evans even managed to take his mountain bike to Kauai by taking it apart and packing it into a box. "It would have cost over $200 in a bike box, but I got a free box from a bike shop, took the bike apart, checked it [on the airplane] as over-sized luggage for $135."

When Amy arrived on Kauai, she rented a car for two weeks until she purchased a used vehicle she found for sale on Craigslist.

## EMPLOYMENT:

Timing was everything in Evans and Amy's relocation. Evans was deeply involved in writing a memoir about his grandfather, so he needed to finish up family interviews before leaving Michigan. However, Amy needed to leave quickly for Kauai because, as a massage therapist, she was required to take an additional class to obtain Hawaii licensure. So Amy left Michigan about a month after the purchase of her airline ticket. That way, she wouldn't miss the start date of the massage class in Kauai. Evans stayed behind.

> Timing was everything in Evans and Amy's relocation.

Prior to leaving the mainland, Amy and Evans applied for a farmhand position on the Worldwide Opportunities on Organic Farms website (http://www.wwoofusa.org/) and were both chosen for a position in Wainiha on the North Shore of Kauai. Amy committed to working on the farm for 20 hours a week until she found another job, and then the hours would be reduced to 10. In exchange, Amy was provided with a bedroom in a house, fruit from the farm, and $200 a month. Evans arrived two months later to visit Amy but only for two weeks. He tried the farming but soon realized he was not cut out for that type of hard labor.

While Amy was busy working 20 hours a week on the farm, she was also attending school to complete the massage class. Upon finishing the class and becoming licensed, she reduced her hours at the farm to 10 a week and began providing massages for income. In addition, Amy cleaned houses and did babysitting to make ends meet.

When Evans arrived permanently on Kauai five months later, he began applying for jobs but decided not to pursue his previous pastoral aspirations. He found ads on Craigslist for writing jobs and was hired to write a few articles for the magazine *Hawaii Traveler* (http://www.myhawaiitraveler.com/). Evans also began taking classes to obtain his substitute-teaching certificate and recently applied at Princeville Ranch for a seasonal part-time position helping with tours.

## HOUSING:

To take full advantage of housing options due to the scarcity of rentals on Kauai, Amy opted to work on the organic farm that provided housing, a little food, and $200 per month. She stayed employed and lived at that farm until Evans arrived permanently later.

When Evans visited Amy prior to his permanent move, they asked around about available housing. "People said to advertise myself," Evans said. As a result, he placed ads on Craigslist and *Heartbeat of Kauai* for housing leads. "Someone contacted us about pet sitting for six weeks in Kapahi. We started taking care of two dogs and three goats," said Evans. He only had to stay at the farm with Amy for a week until their pet- and house-sitting job started.

The pet sitting was ideal for Evans because he could still have time to work on his book. "We had free rent and utilities . . . the woman let us use her car, too. It was fairly ideal . . . but the dogs were needy. I never really left them. But they were great dogs . . . needed a lot of attention. And we cleaned goat stalls!"

View of the Makaleha Mountains from the home where Evans and his wife house sat

Knowing this housing situation would only last six weeks, Evans immediately began searching for his and Amy's next residence. "Housing prices were up even from the previous summer. In six months there was an increase from $800 or $900 to $1000 for a one-bedroom apartment. But we were also looking on the North Shore where housing is more scarce," Evans said.

Evans's housing limit of $1100 per month made the search even more difficult. In addition, he and Amy didn't want to commit to a long-term lease. They searched for month-to-month rental options instead. "We tried for a $1300 [per month] two-bedroom place but someone else rented [it]." Ironically, Evans and Amy attended a party at that same property a few weeks later. Evans concluded, "You can't burn any bridges."

Along the way and before vacating the temporary house-sitting location, Evans heard through a friend about a large house with cabins on a property that was another organic farm. "It had no plumbing . . . one room . . . a hundred square feet with a loft bed for $600 per month on a month-to-month basis in Kapahi. It had one extension cord where we could charge phones and have a lamp. There was an outdoor shower and toilet that was shared [and] a large common kitchen." The price and terms were right so Evans and Amy moved in for about six weeks while continuing the search for another property. Evans confessed that it was glorified camping. "There was no privacy. Shared space. The community didn't have rules. There were domestic disputes. It was no good for long term."

> "Were we just another white mainland couple looking for housing? We felt very much like outsiders to Kauai. We were not sure if this was going to work out."

While paying rent at the temporary one-room cabin, Amy and Evans did another pet-sit for 10 days in Kilauea that paid $20 per day with no rent or utility costs. But they still desperately needed permanent housing. "We kept getting on Craigslist, but the possibilities kept falling through. I was getting frustrated," he admitted. "Were we just another white mainland couple looking for housing? We felt very much like outsiders to Kauai. We were not sure if this was going to work out."

As Evans and Amy continued to advertise themselves as good renters on Craigslist, they received an offer from a landlord to rent a small cabin in Wainiha at $1300 per month. However, they quickly decided it was too far from everything with only one vehicle to share.

Another offer arrived to rent a studio in Kilauea for $1200 per month including utilities, but the landlord wouldn't agree to a month-to-month lease, and the property was due to be placed on the real estate market shortly. The offer seemed a little shaky to Evans. "It was unclear. All word of mouth . . . no lease [to sign]." It made Evans wary, but he and Amy decided to move forward. However, one week before they moved in, they received a lease to sign noting a higher rent of $1400 a month, which the owner claimed was initially a miscalculation of utility costs. Regardless, Evans and Amy, without any other choices, agreed to the price and moved in. But that stay was short lived.

After living in the studio in Kilauea for less than two months, Evans and Amy decided to move on again. At this writing, they gave their notice to vacate the studio to move into a two-bedroom house in Princeville for $2000 a month plus about $400 a month in utility costs. The owner of the Princeville home currently rents out one of the bedrooms to tourists, which Evans and Amy will continue to do to make ends meet. Their goal is to rent out the other bedroom every day of the month in an effort to cover at least half of their monthly rent and utility costs.

> The offer seemed a little shaky to Evans. "It was unclear. All word of mouth . . . no lease [to sign]."

## SCHOOLING:

Amy attended Golden Lotus Studio (http://www.goldenlotuskauai.org/) in Kapaa to finish the one class required to obtain her Hawaii massage certification. Evans believed the cost was between $300 and $500, and the class took eight weeks during the evening to complete.

Since Evans wanted to become certified to be a substitute teacher in the Hawaii public schools, he first had to arrange an interview with a school principal in order to obtain a letter of approval recommending him. According to Evans, substitute teachers also need a four-year college degree. He called a local high school and easily set up an appointment with the secretary. After his interview with the principal, and with the letter of approval in hand, Evans delivered it to the Kauai Community School offices at Kauai High School in Lihue, the school that provided the certification classes. According to Evans, the certification is completed over a weekend at the school and concludes with a two-hour exam for a total cost of $70. He added that the class is only offered during the month of May. More information can be found through the Hawaii Department of Education (http://www.hawaiipublicschools.org/).

> Evans claimed that getting on a school's list is more than just paperwork. "You have to work your way into relationships."

When Evans becomes certified to be a substitute teacher, he will have to visit different schools in order to be added to their list of substitute teachers. He will earn $150–$165 each day he substitutes and said that the pay varies depending on what kind of college degree the applicant possesses. Evans claimed that getting on a school's list is more than just paperwork. "You have to work your way into relationships."

## ACTIVITIES:

Working part-time affords Evans time for outdoor activities. He often kayaks in the Hanalei and Wailua Rivers and on some of the lesser-known rivers like Kalihiwai and Kilauea Streams on the North Shore and Kealia Stream behind Kealia Beach north of Kapaa. All are a 30- to 60-minute paddle up river. Evans has not yet kayaked on the ocean because he wants to have a hardtop kayak first. "Maybe Anini [Beach]—it's fairly safe."

Evans loves hiking and has frequented the North Shore trails and Waimea Canyon, but he has so many favorite hikes, he can't just name one! "Sleeping Giant is really cool . . . incredible views." He also loves the Alakai Swamp Trail in Kokee State Park. "The interior has great views of *the wettest spot on Earth*."

Evans found a great five-mile mountain biking loop, Wai Koa Loop, in Wai Koa Plantation in Kilauea. He claimed this is private land, and bikers are required to sign a waiver at the entrance gate or at the entrance behind Kauai Mini Golf. The waiver states you will agree to obey the rules and stay on the trail. "Halfway there is a dam, picnic area, and a swimming area."

Evans mountain biking among young mahogany trees on the Wai Koa Loop Trail in Kilauea

The East Shore bike path is also one of Evans's favorite. "It's a seven-mile (one-way) path. It begins in Kapaa and goes north to Kealia Beach, then to Donkey Beach, but the only way to get to Donkey Beach is to go all the way to Anahola via unpaved trails. They plan to pave it [north] to Anahola and [south] to Lihue but probably won't."

Evans's favorite place to swim is Anini Beach, but he also loves the Salt Pond Beach Park on the south side of Hanapepe. "It's a traditional place for Hawaiians to gather salt—you're not allowed to go to the pond itself. Salt Pond Park is ideal for swimming—good for families with kids . . . no waves, undertows, or riptides."

## SOCIALIZATION AND INTEGRATION:

Since Evans loves outdoor activities, it is no surprise that he meets others that way. He found a basketball team to play with at the Kilauea Neighborhood Center on the North Shore. "After games, there's a social aspect . . . we grill at the park with other families. It's been really nice."

Connecting through Facebook has yielded many friendships, but Evans warns that becoming *friends* on Facebook is a different process on Kauai. "After you become friends [in person], they will tell you later to go to their Facebook page."

> Evans warns that becoming *friends* on Facebook is a different process on Kauai. "After you become friends [in person], they will tell you later to go to their Facebook page."

After connecting with others through Facebook, Evans started getting invitations to activities and events. "There are different Kauai Facebook groups . . . it's a resource to keep in touch . . . to learn of events and gatherings."

Evans joined a Facebook group of kayakers and hikers. "There are no fees . . . all volunteers. I get emails about one time a week. It's a neat way to plug in."

According to Evans, the Meetup website (http://www.meetup.com/) is popular for middle-aged and retired people. He suggested that the website is helpful, "even if you're just traveling and you'd like to find someone to go hiking."

## HELPFUL RESOURCES:

Besides Craigslist, Amy searched an island-specific website, *Heartbeat of Kauai* (http://www.heartbeatofkauai.com/), used to advertise services, jobs, housing, and goods. "It's a resource for alternative people . . . warm, fuzzy people," Evans shared.

## LIKES:

Evans loves the weather on Kauai and the beautiful outdoorsy things to do. "If you don't like [the weather], then wait five minutes and it will change or drive 10 minutes up the road to different weather."

The smallness of the island is something else Evans enjoys. "The resorts feel separate and [you] forget they're even there. There are no high-rises . . . definitely lots of tourists . . . a good mix of locals. You meet people more than once. Kauai's a small enough place where you always run into them." Evans claimed he even sees tourists over and over again.

A view of Ke'e Beach from the Kalalau Trail, a popular hike on the North Shore of Kauai

Reflecting on his former pastoral career, Evans admitted he enjoys the anonymity of not being a pastor. "When [people] find out I'm a pastor, they close down and they won't be open." Since Evans no longer declares he is a pastor (because he no longer pastors a church), he admitted he hears more interesting stories, especially when he picks up hitchhikers!

## DISLIKES:

The expense of living on Kauai has been difficult for Evans and Amy, but the real struggle has been with the carefree attitude of the island residents. "It's hard not to plan. They're averse to planning . . . it's a surfing culture." On the flip side, Evans enjoys the slower pace of life on the island.

The wildlife is a lot different from what Evans and Amy have experienced in Michigan. "There are lots of feral cats. There was a herd of 20–30 in downtown Lihue!" But Evans is more disturbed by the roosters. "They're everywhere!" He combats the noise by sleeping with earplugs.

Evans noticed two different cultures on the island: the *haoles* (originally meaning a foreigner; now with an added meaning of being a Caucasian), and the local Hawaiians who are *somewhat detached from newcomers,* he claimed. "They keep their distance because so many people come and go."

## BEST MOMENT:

Especially beautiful, according to Evans, are the sunsets viewed from Ke'e Beach on the North Shore. He recalled one of the first times he and Amy watched one. "There were a lot of people. It was cool for us. Everyone else was a tourist. We live here and can come back any time! It was a very cool feeling."

## REGRETS:

Evans admitted that Amy's used car purchase during her first weeks on the island was his biggest regret. The car has had a lot of mechanical problems. He would have liked to buy a new car if they had been able to afford one.

Overall Evans declared, "I like how it all went down. We were blessed with an abundance of savings and it has been our saving grace. Without it, we would have had to leave already or would be in a different living situation . . . or probably making things work on the farm."

## ADAPTATION:

Trying to adapt to the relaxed nature of the island has been tough for Evans. "People are not as exact here. Contracts are used but not

Evans "planking" on a post in Kapahi with the Kalalea Mountain Range of Anahola in the background

always signed immediately. There's an *Aloha Spirit* that things will work out." (*Aloha Spirit* means treating people with deep care and respect.) Evans admitted that the incredible wealth on the island is difficult to comprehend as he and Amy struggle daily to survive. "There are tons of incredible beautiful mansions . . . [areas] that are completely inaccessible to us."

## BEST ADVICE:

Evans offered some advice, listed below, for those who are considering a move to Kauai.

- Come with a minimum of three months' savings.

- Consider working on a farm, especially if you're single. It gives you a chance to get the lay of the land.

- Do your research. Kauai is not what it used to be; there's new wealth—and celebrity mansions, especially on the North Shore.

- Be prepared for the exorbitant cost of living. It's comparable to San Francisco or New York City.

- Utilities are five to six times higher than on the mainland, and most places do not have air conditioning.

- It takes time to earn the right to be heard and to prove yourself.

## VERDICT:

Evans and Amy went to Kauai with the focus of making it as long as they could with the hopes of staying for at least one year. "The island can welcome you and things [will be] made apparent within two years." At least that is what Evans has heard.

The new rental in Princeville will determine if Evans and Amy will be able to stay on the island. If the spare bedroom has a lot of vacancy, their stay on Kauai may be limited due to the lack of enough income.

Evans with a giant pomelo on the farm in Kapahi

Angelica describes the Tantalus Mountain Loop trail as a *mountainous, jungle-ly place.*

**Angelica and Rody as mermaids**
*Courtesy of Mermaids of Hawaii (http://www.mermaidsofhawaii.com/)*

# CASE #47279: ALL GOOD THINGS COME TO THOSE WHO WAIT

**Perpetrator(s):** Angelica (28), Rody (42)
**Accomplice(s):** None
**Time In Hawaii:** 1.5 Years
**Island:** Oahu

## BACKGROUND:

At only 10 years old, Angelica began planning her future move to Hawaii. After vacationing dozens of times with her family to visit extended family on the island of Oahu, she knew it was destined to be her home. That's why when she met Rody, she immediately made it clear that they would someday relocate to Oahu. Although he didn't quite understand her need to move to Hawaii, he agreed.

Angelica's goal was to *come home* before the age of 30. "That's exactly what I did, but I was three years early!" Angelica made it to Hawaii at 27 years old. Educated in accounting with a work history in publishing, she was a good planner and had a knack for crunching numbers. This resulted in Angelica securing a job while still living on the mainland. Angelica and Rody's lease was almost up on their northern California apartment, and within two weeks of obtaining her new job, she and Rody moved. Angelica started her job immediately upon arrival to their new home on the island of Oahu.

## FINANCES:

Having saved money for her Hawaii move since she was 17 years old, Angelica was as ". . . well prepared as anyone my age could be," she confessed. Though Rody didn't have quite the same master plan, he agreed to contribute all of his salary to the savings account to pursue Angelica's dream.

Angelica's and Rody's diligent saving enabled them to purchase a home during their first year in Hawaii. However, she wonders how they will save money to buy a larger house someday when they start a family. She sometimes worries about not being able to upgrade their housing when necessary because they have used the majority of their savings already. "We are still able to save a little, which we put on the principal mortgage balance, which is kind of like a savings," she said.

## TRAVEL AND SHIPPING:

Since Angelica's extended family was already on Oahu, she found moving fairly easy. She and Rody only moved what they could carry, two bags per person. Flying Hawaiian Airlines, they bought two one-way tickets for $700 each. Since it was summer, the tickets were expensive.

Rody and Angelica owned one vehicle and had Matson (http://www.matson.com/) in Oakland ship it to Oahu for $1100. Matson *did a good job,* Angelica claimed. She and Rody were without a car for a month in Oahu, but Angelica's uncle was very helpful and became their chauffeur until their car arrived. This saved them money on a car rental.

Missing her belongings, Angelica recalled, "I have a bunch of stuff at my parent's house in Sacramento that I will probably bring over little by little." She wished she had brought more personal items to Oahu like her stuffed animals and her diaries.

## EMPLOYMENT:

Having a Master of Arts degree in accounting and a Bachelor of Arts degree in Japanese led Angelica to search for a job requiring fluency in Japanese. She applied for a job requiring bilingualism in English and Japanese and was hired while still living on the mainland, which left her and Rody only two weeks to get to Oahu.

Soon after arriving and starting her job at a local college, Angelica realized that it was not what she wanted, so she soon left her new employer and hurriedly took a different job. That job turned out to be the wrong one for many reasons, but Angelica was thankful for the experience. "It led me to do lots of other things that are more fun," like some tutoring, writing, and graphic art. Angelica currently is a ghostwriter of online math problems, has her own animal fashion brand called HakuAi, and sells items at dog shows and dog grooming salons. She also provides company-branding services for various businesses in addition to her primary job as an on-call accountant.

> Angelica admits that they ". . . work crazy hours to make ends meet."

Rody has found steady employment through Tempco, a temporary employment agency, in the area of retail. Since he is not fluent in English, he is limited as to what jobs he can secure. Angelica admits that they ". . . work crazy hours to make ends meet." They were only unemployed a couple of months total but were able to use money from their savings account to get by.

## HOUSING:

Angelica's planning didn't stop with finances. Her aunt was *super helpful*. However, Angelica shared, "Some people think that connections are everything, but they're not." She and Rody had made arrangements to stay with her aunt's friend who owned a small apartment complex. Unfortunately, the friend changed her mind when Angelica and Rody arrived, and they were forced to stay in a hotel and were faced with unexpected expenses.

> "Some people think that connections are everything, but they're not."

After four days in the hotel, they hastily secured housing that Angelica admits *probably wasn't right,* which resulted in a less-than-pleasant experience. Angelica recalled, "We rented a house in the McCully neighborhood toward the mountain by Ala-Wai," which she describes as a *dirty canal with flesh-eating bacteria, a scuzzy area, really dirty.* On top of it, Angelica claimed their rental was infested with bedbugs, which the landlord tried to blame on them. "I wasn't going to take crap from a landlord anymore," Angelica said. She and Rody packed up their belongings and impulsively purchased a house.

Purchasing a house spontaneously had its repercussions as well. It consumed the remaining savings that Angelica and Rody worked so long to attain, and they bought in the same McCully neighborhood that they had rented in, and it wasn't a neighborhood they liked very much. There is no yard, which will pose a problem when they have children. They also bought at the top of their budget and only got a two-bedroom home. "I freak out thinking how we're ever going to move up," Angelica disclosed.

## SCHOOLING:

N/A

## ACTIVITIES:

Angelica has joined classes including crafts, dance, and hula and they are held at others' houses. Her aunt has helped her integrate with others in this way. She also hikes with her family in places like Tantalus, which she describes as a *mountainous, jungle-ly place.* Angelica's favorite trail is Makapu'u because it has beautiful panoramic views of Oahu.

View of the lighthouse on Makapu'u Trail.

Over a year into their new life on Oahu, Angelica and Rody work many hours and have only gone to the beach about five times. "I would like to go to the beach more often, but we are so busy trying to make ends meet," explains Angelica, even though she and Rody live only a 10-minute walk to the closest beach.

## SOCIALIZATION AND INTEGRATION:

Angelica meets people easily, but Rody isn't as fortunate. "I feel like I integrate well because I'm always uprooted and I'm friendly. I make an effort. Rody is more introverted because of the language barrier, and his personality is quiet."

Angelica also participates in some classes and has met others through the classes. She is outgoing and has gained good friends just by walking in her neighborhood and striking up conversations. "It's like anywhere else," she shared. "People will generally treat you how you treat them."

## HELPFUL RESOURCES:

Since the move wasn't exactly planned, Angelica didn't do much research prior to moving. "I found a job on Craigslist and everything else was handed down to me from my relatives."

## LIKES:

Angelica and Rody love the weather in Hawaii. "It's warm now," Angelica shared. "I don't do well with the cold, and by cold I mean temperatures less than 75 degrees. I'm free to dress the way that I feel is normal, and I don't get sick as often." She is happy not to have to wear three jackets to stay warm in 60-degree temperatures like she did in northern California.

Angelica and Rody on the North Shore of Oahu

On the bright side, it is easy to find work on Oahu, *even though it may not be good work,* Angelica admitted. "The hiring process in general seems quick and efficient here as compared to California, and there isn't as much real competition for a person reasonably well qualified for a mediocre-paying position because most of the best and brightest have left the state for higher paying jobs elsewhere."

## DISLIKES:

Angelica misses the amenities from the Bay Area, like her free pottery classes, Trader Joe's, and Whole Foods Market. "Whole Foods is too expensive on Oahu," Angelica shares. "I also want a bigger house. I don't want to live in McCully forever," she continues.

Angelica *strongly dislikes* the quarantine laws in Hawaii. After recently purchasing a dog from California, Angelica claims the animal suffered severe trauma in quarantine after it was shipped. She is adamant that if she ever purchases another animal, she intends to be living on the mainland so she doesn't have to go through the experience again.

"The nasty attitude of the drivers is Rody's biggest gripe about living in Honolulu, other than the cost of living. Drivers are jerks and will honk or shout at pedestrians who clearly have the right of way," Angelica explained, frustrated.

## BEST MOMENT:

Although Angelica's grandmother has passed away, her best moments are linked to her grandmother and the home Angelica visited during her childhood years. Although Angelica's uncle currently lives in her grandmother's home, she hopes to gain ownership of it someday. "Pretty much whenever I go visit my grandma's house . . . that's home to me."

## REGRETS:

Angelica's biggest regret is that she didn't move sooner because she could have gotten more house for her money. She knows that someday she will look back and say, "Wow, I can't believe I once got a tiny house for a mere half million! Unreal!"

The lack of funds necessary to travel keeps Angelica separated from her close-knit family. "I miss my family and friends, but I'm an optimist. I was kept away from Hawaii; now I'm kept away from California. Hopefully, someday we'll all be together in Hawaii."

## ADAPTATION:

Angelica and Rody's move went fairly well in her opinion, and she insists they will stay on Oahu. "My husband is happy to be by himself." She feels like she's home. "At least I won't spend my life yearning to go home."

## BEST ADVICE:

Angelica's and Rody's suggestions, listed below, don't include planning or traveling, but are focused on adapting to island life.

- Buy a house as soon as you can if you know you're going to stay. Even if you're only going to stay a couple years, buy because you will make a profit when you leave.

- If you are a colorful dresser or you like to wear makeup, don't work downtown. You will be harassed and criticized for not fitting in.

- Don't ever buy a bike because it WILL get stolen. Even if you chain it up in the middle of the day and take the seat off, it will get stolen. Some people buy a kick scooter that you can fold up and take indoors with you.

- Rody's co-workers have warned him about discrimination against Asians and claim if your skin is pale, guard your purse with your life and always look over your shoulder.

◆ Don't think you can survive in Hawaii without sweaters and jackets. The air conditioning in most indoor settings is brutal.

## VERDICT:

Although Angelica loves the weather, she and Rody have recently felt like they *have kind of had it* with the negatives of Oahu. With the traffic concerns, the high cost of living, and the negative attitude of the people, Angelica and Rody aren't guaranteeing they will stay.

Brandi's favorite hike is in Waipio Valley. "It is gorgeous."

Brandi, Jason and their daughter

**Perpetrator(s):** Brandi (36), Jason (42)
**Accomplice(s):** Daughter (4)
**Time In Hawaii:** 7 Years
**Island:** Big Island

## BACKGROUND:

Growing up in California and living in Hollywood while she worked in the film industry, Brandi had had her share of excitement. But a simple wedding invitation to the Big Island from her best friend, along with a round-trip plane ticket, changed Brandi's life forever.

Brandi was not prepared for what happened next. "I landed on the rock, saw my guitar on the tarmac, and said, *Here I am, God. It's where I want to stay.*" She knew immediately that the Big Island was going to be her home. She quickly called her family to tell them she was staying, and it was difficult for them to understand. "They all thought I was crazy!"

One year later, Jason walked into Brandi's life at Lulu's, a now out-of-business bar in Kona. He had just arrived on the island for a construction job. About two years later and after many attempts to date Brandi, she finally agreed and went out with Jason. An engagement, pregnancy, and wedding soon followed.

Seven years, a wedding, and one baby girl later, Brandi and Jason live happily in Kona on the Big Island of Hawaii.

## FINANCES:

Since Brandi had a round-trip ticket and no plans to stay on the Big Island, she did not plan for the sudden expense of island living. Besides spending money for her vacation, she was penniless. On day three she secured two jobs, one as a bartender and one as a server, which produced income instantly. "That's how I got through life," Brandi said comfortably.

## TRAVEL AND SHIPPING:

Since Brandi's plane ticket was covered, she didn't have any travel expenses. All of her possessions were already in storage because she was between residences on the mainland when she left for the wedding on the Big Island. She had just sold her car to a relative and had planned on purchasing another one when she returned from vacation. Therefore staying in Hawaii *was easy*. She bought a moped and kept it for a few years until she could afford a car. Jason brought over his Kia Sportage when he originally arrived, and now they share a few vehicles as a family.

Arriving in Hawaii with only enough money for a vacation, Brandi reflected, "I used to battle with the letting go of all of the material things I had. I came here with a suitcase and a guitar, and all other things were left in a 10x10 storage unit in California, but I never needed it; it was just stuff, [but] you get more stuff."

## EMPLOYMENT:

Brandi worked as a server and bartender for most of her time on the island, but is now a full-time mom. She also recently started a babysitting company (http://www.bigislandbabysitting.com/), which has experienced some success. However, she has found some competitors bad-mouthing her business to hotels, one of her primary sources of business, which she was surprised to hear.

Jason spent quite a while as a stay-at-home dad because the construction business completely died on the Big Island. However, he is now back to work in the construction field, which allows Brandi to stay home with their daughter.

## HOUSING:

Although Brandi traveled around the whole island prior to securing housing, she prefers Kona. "I love Kona because it's most like California. I like the Kona people, where you know everyone, but there are still lots of people who come and go, like the tourists, and cruise ships." The Hilo side is nice too, Brandi admitted, but ". . . it's very local and just feels different, and it just isn't Kona."

> "I love Kona because it's most like California . . ."

Brandi stayed with her wedding friend the first week on the Big Island, but soon landed a room rental in Kona with three others referred by her friend. Within six months Brandi was able to move out and secure a studio for herself for the next two years just a mile from Magic Sands Beach in Kona. When Brandi and Jason were ready to move in together, they found a rental house *just steps* from Magic Sands Beach, where they still reside.

## SCHOOLING:

Already thinking about kindergarten for her four-year-old daughter, Brandi is leaning toward homeschooling. "I have heard good and bad about the schools. I just think I would have enjoyed it as a child and learning by reading and doing." She is currently looking at preschools and is considering the Salvation Army, which is $500 per month for part-time care.

## ACTIVITIES:

Besides Brandi's love for the guitar, she does get to frequent the beach almost daily but stated, "It is draining to get all sandy and clean up a four-year-old, but we do our best to go often." She also has paddle boarded in the past but hasn't had time lately to pursue it. The family also enjoys going to Queen's Bath, an open-air lava tube that is filled with cold, fresh water, on the northern Kona coast by Kiholo Bay, and Brandi's favorite hike is in Waipio Valley. "It is gorgeous," she marveled.

## SOCIALIZATION AND INTEGRATION:

Although Brandi hoped joining a church would help with acclimation to the island, a church she and her family attended in Kona was not the right fit for them.

On the other hand, Brandi claimed, "It's easy to befriend locals and mainlanders . . ." because they are very friendly, especially in Kona. It's also easy to meet people out-and-about, including at the beach, she said. "Everyone's happy . . . they're in Hawaii. They can't help but be happy even though they are going through hard times."

## HELPFUL RESOURCES:

Brandi said that using Facebook is common on the Big Island, even for buying and selling of items. Craigslist is also helpful and items are generally priced well.

## LIKES:

The Big Island is a *rough, raw, beautiful island,* Brandi revealed. Besides enjoying the people on the island, Brandi spends a lot of time at the ocean and takes advantage of the relaxing island lifestyle by enjoying the beach and the scenery and by getting together with friends. *Just being able to go to the mountains to see the stars* helps Brandi to appreciate the island. She also likes collecting shells from around the island.

## DISLIKES:

According to Brandi the availability of medical services on the Big Island is not up to par; however all top-notch services are available on Oahu. When it came time for her baby's delivery, the North Hawaii Community Hospital in Waimea was not Brandi's first choice. "The women's health center is for low-income [families], but the medical care seemed okay." She would have much rather had a home birth, but Jason was adamant about a hospital birth.

Brandi is still adjusting to the difficulty of finding things she needs on the island. Things that are available on the mainland are not available on the Big Island. However, Brandi claimed that anything is available on the island of Oahu.

Brandi thinks having to pick and choose when to return to the mainland is tough because of coordinating time off from several jobs. Having extra money set aside to attend a funeral, wedding, or a new birth would help to ease the financial difficulty of traveling off-island.

## BEST MOMENT:

Knowing she was already home on the Big Island, her feelings were confirmed when she met her husband. "Knowing he was the one and

having my child were [my] two best moments [on the Big Island],"
Brandi shared. Staying on the Big Island would not have been possible if it hadn't been for Jason coming into her life.

## REGRETS:

Only recently has Brandi had regrets because of her family's medical
issues on the mainland. The birth of her niece and her grandmother's
death were also difficult to cope with from a distance. However,
Brandi's desire to live in a foreign-like location fuels her desire to
stay in Hawaii.

Brandi concluded, "Life is an adventure, and I feel adventurous,
and for that I have no regrets, but missing the loved ones leads me
to question [that sometimes]."

## ADAPTATION:

Brandi has befriended many
people in Hawaii and has felt
at home for quite some time.
"Definitely, I've adapted,"
Brandi said enthusiastically.
"I hate it when I have to leave
and love coming home to the
Big Island."

Hawaii has its downside
too, Brandi shared. The island
Brandi, Jason and their daughter
is beautiful, but Brandi warned,
"Beauty has its ugly." People arrive to Hawaii and leave just as quickly.
She and Jason are working hard to avoid being those people.

## BEST ADVICE:

Brandi warned if you are close to your family then you need to understand that you may not see them again. "You'd think living in Hawaii . . . *Who doesn't want to come to Hawaii,* but honestly things come up, life happens, and tomorrow sometimes turns to a dream and history." Because of the long-distance struggles, Brandi doesn't see her family often. Jason's mother even moved to the Big Island to be with her new family.

In addition, Brandi suggested the following, along with a warning, listed below.

- Pick an area of the island that is pleasing to your heart.

- Have extra money set aside to travel back home when needed.

- If you are not meant to be here, the island will make you leave; whether it's with an illness or an injury, you will be sent home.

## VERDICT:

Even though her family on the mainland wants her to move back, Brandi insisted, "This is home to me." But she is always aware that God's plan may be different. "My husband wants to stay, but we might try another island someday, like Maui." Only God knows.

Makena Beach is Conni's favorite place to have a picnic ". . . because it's more pristine and serene," than other parts of the island.

Conni at Four Seasons Resort

# CASE #49981: FREE SPIRIT

**Perpetrator(s):** Conni (51)
**Accomplice(s):** None
**Time In Hawaii:** 5 Months
**Island:** Maui

. . . . . . . . . . . . . . . . . . . . . . . . . . . . . . . . . . . . . . . . . . . . . .

## BACKGROUND:

Conni always believed she had a *spiritual slant* to follow her own path in life. Insisting that the metaphor for her life was *The Wizard of Oz*, she followed that inner urging all over the United States. From her hometown in Wisconsin, that urging led her to several states including Florida, Arizona, California, and Hawaii. The strongest draw was to the tiny town of Sedona in Arizona.

No stranger to Maui, Conni had relocated to the island once before, nearly 14 years ago. That residency lasted five years until she was tugged back to Sedona. After a year in Sedona, Conni spent six years in northern California then went on to spend her last year on the mainland in Tucson, Arizona. That familiar longing to relocate surfaced again, and this time it was to return to Hawaii.

Conni's confirmation came to her in an unconventional way. "I was always good at listening. I got a tap on the shoulder to move [again to Maui]. I waited six to 12 months for clarity." After some doors opened, including having a job offer from a restaurant and free housing, Conni believed that was her cue. "I had enough [air] miles for a one-way ticket." Four months later she arrived on Maui for the second time.

## FINANCES:

Conni was living on a month-to-month basis at the time of her relocation to Maui with nothing tying her down. She had saved about $4000 prior to her move. With her free plane ticket, free housing, and a job already secured, Conni didn't have to worry much about money.

Conni spent about $1400 traveling to visit her family prior to moving to Maui, and she spent some of her savings to ship boxes to the island. After selling her car, she landed on Maui with about $2600 remaining.

Unfortunately, Conni received some bad news about her promised job on Maui right before she was due to leave for Hawaii. "The restaurant had been open 16 years, and two weeks before I left Tucson the restaurant closed." This bad news added an element of urgency to Conni's need for work.

## TRAVEL AND SHIPPING:

Conni confessed to having few belongings so it was fairly easy to pack up and move. "I went through my stuff, sold things on Craigslist, donated to Goodwill. I shipped seven apple boxes of my things to my friend's home on Maui. I can always buy stuff at estate sales or garage sales." She spent $400 shipping her personal items to Maui using media mail, which Conni claimed was the cheapest way to ship.

Conni decided not to ship her vehicle to Maui because the cost was too expensive. Instead she sold it on Craigslist prior to relocating.

The sale of her vehicle spurred her to begin searching for a motorcycle to have on Maui. Through research, Conni realized that the type of motorcycle she wanted would be less expensive in Hawaii, and even cheaper on the Big Island.

While still on the mainland, Conni began searching Craigslist to find the motorcycle of her dreams. She found *the one* on the Big Island and purchased it from a private party for $1900 using PayPal, an online payment service (https://www.paypal.com/), to pay for it. The private seller then delivered the motorcycle to Kiser Motorcycles in Kona, which crated it for $150 and arranged for delivery to the Maui shipyard for another $150. The motorcycle shop employee ensured that the cycle was there and in good shape and verified the title and other papers were present. When the seller confirmed payment had been received from Conni, the key and title were handed over to Kiser Motorcycles and they, in turn, mailed them to Conni while she awaited the motorcycle delivery to Maui.

Conni's motorcycle after arrival to the shipyard

Since Conni didn't have the motorcycle immediately upon arriving to Maui, her friend picked her up at the airport. The following day the friend had to leave the island for work, and Conni used her car until the motorcycle arrived. She took the bus, which only cost two dollars, to the mall in Kahului and walked a few blocks to the shipyard with the papers in hand to pick up her new motorcycle. Armed with a screwdriver, she and a couple shipyard workers opened the crate. "[They] wouldn't even accept a tip! It's the Aloha Spirit."

## EMPLOYMENT:

Conni's previous stay on Maui resulted in friendships that were maintained over the prior 14 years. These friends helped her with this relocation. Her former employer, a restaurant manager, offered her a job upon her return to the island. As the restaurant closed prior to her arriving on Maui, she immediately started looking for jobs, but soon found that no one was hiring. "For [the] hotel/ restaurant business it's usually best to be on-island before applying because [the companies] want to see your face. [It's] also very competitive; lots of servers/bartenders looking for jobs . . . so you need to be there."

Upon her arrival on Maui, Conni continued to look for jobs, but she was being discerning with her applications. "September through November is not a good season [to look for jobs]. It's a slow time of year." Conni did take some proactive measures to gain employment; she changed her phone number to a Hawaii number immediately upon arrival.

> "September through November is not a good season [to look for jobs]. It's a slow time of year."

Two months later, Conni secured a job at a restaurant, and shortly thereafter she was rehired by another employer she had during her previous time on Maui, working in the banquet department at the Four Seasons Resort Maui. "I interviewed at a lot of places . . . at the job fair . . . so many people are trying for the same job."

Unfortunately, after only six shifts at the Four Seasons, Conni fell and broke her shoulder while working at the other restaurant. She is now unable to work any jobs and is on disability, which pays her 66 percent of her income including tips. She said she is still able to meet her monthly obligations because the disability income is not taxed, so it's almost like she is getting her regular paycheck with taxes taken out.

## HOUSING:

During Conni's previous stay on Maui, she befriended another restaurant employee who is now a flight attendant. The flight attendant was looking for someone to live in an *ohana* (meaning family but often used to reference a guesthouse) on her property in Wailea and to also take care of her cat while she was away working. Conni's only obligation was to provide basic care for the property and pay half of the utilities, which amounts to about $200 per month. Conni insisted, "God laid it out for me."

Conni revealed she ". . . loves living [and] working in the Wailea area because it's very nice, clean, and not as touristy or congested as Kihei or Lahaina or some other areas."

## SCHOOLING:

N/A

## ACTIVITIES:

"I love to be in nature . . . hike . . . hop on [my] motorcycle. I drove around the backside of the island. I love spontaneity," Conni emphasized. Her favorite place to have a picnic or go to the beach is Makena ". . . because it is more pristine and serene," than other parts of the island.

Conni has also kayaked at Kamaole Beaches I & II in Kihei and at Makena Landing Beach Park in South Maui. She snorkeled at Makena Landing and at the Fish Bowl, also in South Maui, which she admits used to be a great place but now doesn't have as many fish.

Conni's motorcycle taking a rest on a drive to Hana

Conni recently went whale watching with the Pacific Whale Foundation at *reasonable prices*. "Saw lots of whales, babies, males fighting over a female." She even saw a whale breaching out of the water just five yards from the boat. "I don't have to be in the water . . . just by it."

Connie remembered also that the Maui Arts and Cultural Center in Kahului has ". . . many great shows and classes."

## SOCIALIZATION AND INTEGRATION:

Conni meets others through the restaurant business, which she thinks is the *natural way* to meet others. She also joined Unity Church in Wailuku, where she goes occasionally. Conni acknowledged only having a handful of close friends on the island and admitted she really likes to be alone. "I don't go out of my way to meet others. I believe *like attracts like*, and if it's meant to be, then it will be." She is also not in any hurry to have a life partner but confesses that she finally feels ready. "I've lived a good single life . . . the right person will be brought to me."

## HELPFUL RESOURCES:

Conni has used Craigslist successfully for many things, including searching for a vehicle and jobs.

Through Facebook, Conni found a very helpful website that she highly recommends for everyone, https://nextdoor.com/. Any neighborhood can join, according to Conni. "It's where neighbors share important information." She once saw that someone in her neighborhood had her mail stolen and wanted to inform everyone. Others often ask for referrals for pest control or landscaping. Once she even saw that someone needed a ride somewhere and then received a referral to a private taxi service that only charged two dollars per mile.

## LIKES:

Conni has a love for people and claims she is very down to earth. "I've lived all over the country . . . [the people on Maui] are not pretentious . . . not materialistic . . . [they're] authentic."

She also is attracted to the *energy* of Maui; it has nature and beauty at its roots. "It's very healing and relaxing. I loved California, but not the materialism or superficiality of it."

Every day Conni is well aware that she is in Hawaii by the Aloha Spirit she experiences, and noticed it vividly the day she picked up her motorcycle at the shipyard. "They wouldn't accept the $5 bill I tried to hand to them. [They] simply treated me as if I were their

An example of the Aloha Spirit at a Hana fruit stand
with payment based on the honor system

sister or friend. They didn't consider for one moment to accept my five dollars."

Conni ascertained, "Hawaii truly does have the Aloha Spirit, and that's more than just a fancy word for hello and goodbye. *Ha* means breath and *alo* means unity. One interpretation of Aloha is 'We breathe the same breath of God and are one.'"

## DISLIKES:

Conni enjoys the weather of Maui but said that Kihei is a *little warm* for her.

"My family is so far away. I love road trips, and I can't hop in the car and go at the last second," Conni said. "It's hard because I feel like I'm in another country. The first time I was here, I felt alone. Lonely. If something goes wrong with my family, I can't jump in the car and go."

Now that Conni is well into her second residency on Maui, she has felt that the loneliness has lifted. "Once life is going, you won't feel that way. I've plugged in and feel at home."

Besides missing her family, Conni doesn't have many complaints. However, finding a centipede crawling on her body in the middle of the night wasn't something that was easy for her! "I suddenly felt something crawling on my arm, and I went to brush it off. As I opened my eyes, I was horrified to see it was a large five-inch long centipede! As I brushed him off, he did bite me!"

Conni confessed that she has only seen a few centipedes over a period of six years on Maui but offered some advice if people do find them inside their houses. "Using tongs you need to twist back and forth to cut their head off . . . cut [it] into several pieces. If you just cut the end or middle . . . they will live and grow more legs. I've heard that some people smash them with a hammer or even put them into a metal can and burn them. You don't want to flush them down the toilet unless you've killed them first!"

There is one more safeguard Conni uses against centipedes. "I buy boric acid insecticidal dust and put some of the powder around all four of the legs of my bed! This gives me peace of mind that I can sleep without worrying about anything crawling on me or biting

> "I buy boric acid insecticidal dust and put some of the powder around all four of the legs of my bed! This gives me peace of mind that I can sleep without worrying about anything crawling on me or biting me!"

me!" Conni purchased the boric acid at a local hardware store and said it is also used for killing roaches and other bugs.

## BEST MOMENT:

Intuition was the cement that sealed Conni's contentment on Maui. "I've had so many beautiful moments," she said, but remembers one big reason why she thinks she was led to Maui. A friend on the island had cancer, and Conni has been able to help her through the difficult treatment process. "That alone would have been worth being here. We are close soul sisters. We have a special connection."

## REGRETS:

Though things didn't always go perfectly, Conni has no regrets and claimed, "Everything happens for a reason." She does wish she had arrived with more money, but she was able to take a long road trip prior to leaving the mainland, and she thinks that was well worth the money. In retrospect, if Conni had known that her financial situation was going to stabilize so quickly she wouldn't have worried so much about it.

## ADAPTATION:

Conni has great respect for the Hawaiian culture. Her church teaches hula and often opens the service by blowing a conch shell.

The diversity of the residents in Hawaii is what makes the islands special. After thinking more carefully, she realized she works with Filipinos and Hawaiians, and it came to her that she didn't even notice the diversity before. "It's neat . . . cool . . . a melting pot."

Conni considers herself very adaptable, which is why she claims she can move anywhere all the time. "I force myself to live in the present moment . . . to surrender control."

## BEST ADVICE:

Conni's advice, listed below, comes from her heart together with a splash of reality.

- ◆ Follow your joy and passion . . . it's there for a reason.

- ◆ Don't let naysayers deter you from following your dream.

- ◆ If you are meant to do it, trust it.

- ◆ Use your head. Go do it, but utilize available resources.

- ◆ Think outside the box; there are more ways to make it work than you think.

- ◆ Rent a room because there are not many apartments available and usually 30+ people are vying for one place.

- ◆ If you have a pet, don't move unless you have a place to live first. It takes you out of the competition for a house.

## VERDICT:

Though Conni loves Maui and feels at home, she also feels at home in Sedona, Arizona. "I will always travel. It depends on the work situation. I'll see what happens over summer with my housing and job. I may move off-season to get a job. Never say never."

Natalie said, "Hawaii surfers are less territorial [compared to Californians] about surfing spots, and there are more abundant breaks. There's a general feeling of aloha here."

# CASE #23918: A "SAXY" GIRL

**Perpetrator(s):** Natalie* (26), Mike* (29)
**Accomplice(s):** 2 Dogs
**Time In Hawaii:** 10 Months
**Island:** Oahu

## BACKGROUND:

Raised by a Hell's Angel, Natalie had no choice but to be a free thinker. Independence was her middle name, so it's no surprise that she graduated college with a dramatic arts degree and is now an aspiring independent filmmaker and photographer in Hawaii. Added to that is Natalie's passion for playing the saxophone. Mike is right alongside Natalie with a history in the surfboard industry and home rehabilitation. Surfing was their passion in northern California, and it remains a significant part of their lives in Hawaii.

Natalie and Mike dreamed of living in Hawaii for three years before the move actually happened. Natalie visited Oahu once in high school for a band performance, and Mike spent a

---

* *Names Have Been Changed.*

year living on Oahu just out of high school. When his employer offered him an opportunity to rehabilitate a recently purchased house on Oahu, he and Natalie jumped at the chance to relocate. Two weeks later, Mike was in Hawaii, and two short weeks after that, Natalie joined him.

As Natalie mused, "With two long boards, three extra large bags, and two angry pit bulls," she and Mike relocated to Hawaii.

## FINANCES:

Due to the short notice, there was little time for financial planning. Natalie and Mike sold their RV, or *nest egg*, to a friend, took their $3000 in savings, and left for Hawaii. They weren't too concerned about money since they were able to move into the house that Mike was rehabilitating for the real estate company. However, once they arrived, the terms of the relocation they had agreed upon were not what they thought, and this resulted in unexpected expenses.

"The budget was unclear. There was an expense account, but we didn't realize our living expenses were included in the expense account for the rehab. We had many unexpected costs quickly," Natalie shared . . . like dog surgery, a vehicle, two tires, and some camera equipment. "There was no money left."

## TRAVEL AND SHIPPING:

Prior to moving to Oahu, Mike and Natalie had a short-term rehabilitation job on Maui. He departed to Maui before Natalie, and she and the two 60-pound dogs followed a few weeks later.

After Mike left California, Natalie had to quickly liquidate everything. She kept some important items in a storage facility in San Diego. These included most of her instruments, bikes, and surfboards, but then she *threw the rest of my life away*, she said.

Natalie couldn't face people digging through her belongings at a garage sale because she was too emotional. Instead, she randomly bundled everything up in garbage bags and gave away the bags. It was the only way she could part with her things, but she did leave a few special instruments, like her saxophone, with a trustworthy friend. "If all things had been shipped," Natalie stated, "the relocation would have been much easier."

Natalie and Mike did ship a small vehicle after finding that most companies estimated the shipping cost between $1500 and $2000. No personal belongings can be placed inside the vehicle, but items can be put inside the shipping container that the vehicle is in.

> If all things had been shipped," Natalie stated, "the relocation would have been much easier."

Natalie found Alaska Airlines to be the best airline for flying with pets. "Their compartments for animal travel are superior to any of the other airlines." She paid $100 per dog to travel in the cargo area of the plane and said, regardless of size, it's that same price. Natalie said that airlines restrict travel for certain breeds during certain months. For instance, all short-nosed breeds aren't allowed to fly during peak summer months. She found it difficult to locate supplies to ship large dogs, such as large dog feeders, waterers, pee pads, and shipping labels, so some items were purchased online through various merchants prior to the relocation.

Natalie warned that upon arrival to the mainland airport for an outbound flight to Hawaii, there is significant wait time for the agriculture department to check in animals. She suggested arriving early for the flight. A final arrival time to the Hawaii airport before 2:00 p.m. allows pets a guaranteed transfer to the animal quarantine facility without the pet owner in attendance, which saves a lot of hassle upon arrival.

## EMPLOYMENT:

Mike's employer, a real estate company, purchased houses in Hawaii that needed to be rehabilitated. He was hired to rehabilitate one of the houses on Maui and subsequently one on Oahu. After two months in Maui, he and Natalie relocated to Oahu to rehabilitate another house. They were given a budget for the rehabilitation along with Mike's weekly salary of $500. In addition, they were promised $35 a day for personal expenses. Unfortunately, upon arrival they found that they would not receive the additional $35 a day, and this produced a hardship for them.

> Natalie confessed to needing a career that involves *traveling and creativity* and believes that Hawaii will fulfill those needs.

Currently Natalie is pursuing her career as a photographer and eventually hopes to move into making personal documentaries. She goes to the beach and solicits business by photographing surfers and then selling the photos. She is already earning $1200 per month from her photography alone. "There are definitely many more surfer photo opportunities here than in California."

Natalie confessed to needing a career that involves *traveling and creativity* and believes that Hawaii will fulfill those needs. "I have always been an adventurer, and I start to rot when I stay in one place too long. I figured moving was less expensive than therapy!"

## HOUSING:

Luckily for Natalie and Mike, his employer handed housing to them. Although they did not have options when it came to housing, they like their neighborhood in Ewa Beach. Their house would normally rent for about $1500 per month. Mike's expense account covers nearly all of their expenses. Moving into a house that needs rehabilitation is not ideal, but it solved the problem of searching for housing.

Ewa Beach is west of Pearl Harbor according to Natalie. "It is a bit rough and depends what street you live on." She also said the closer to the beach, the creepier the area gets. "There are a lot of poor families where family members live in the front yard—one house may have upwards of 15 people living there. It's sad, but they have a lot of love."

Natalie said that on a two-mile street there are probably only three haoles. "Everyone has papaya trees and mango trees. Everyone lives off the land as much as possible." She shared her joy of the unique wildlife on Oahu. "I have a friend on my porch. I call him Mr. Lizard. There are lots of cool things here."

Natalie does warn to stay out of the *Wild West*, the west side of Oahu. She stated that area is the last real refuge that is intensely local. "You have to be careful in the Makaha area; don't leave anything in your car. They don't care whether you're white, Samoan. It doesn't matter; you don't come in their space."

## SCHOOLING:

N/A

## ACTIVITIES:

"Surfing is the tip of the iceberg when it comes to nature around here," Natalie revealed. "Hawaii surfers are less territorial [compared to Californians] about surfing spots, and there are more abundant breaks. There's a general feeling of aloha here."

Natalie confesses to enjoying California surfing more than surfing in Hawaii because of the more regular point breaks and because Hawaii has more shore breaks. Although it's true, she said,

"In California you're surfing in a giant mush bowl of kelp and the water's cold." But she also admits she enjoys Hawaii's much warmer waters, and adds that California surfers are more aggressive but so are the waves, which Natalie enjoyed.

## SOCIALIZATION AND INTEGRATION:

According to Natalie, people are very friendly and talkative and *have a lot of aloha.* "But your socialization depends upon your own friendliness and aloha attitude. As long as you don't go to their hangout spots or say stupid things, you will be treated with aloha."

Natalie remembers a day when she was walking down the street and a neighbor yelled, "Hey girl, you lost?" She responded that she had just moved in down the street. The neighbor told her and Mike to ". . . come have some beer and pork." The neighbor adopted them, according to Natalie. The neighbor always brings them platters of food.

Natalie also places ads on Craigslist to find female surfing buddies. "I am extremely amicable and make friends very, very easy," she offered. "The surfing community all want to know each other."

## HELPFUL RESOURCES:

The relocation notification happened so quickly that Natalie tried researching online but only found tourism information. She said, "I jumped in a pot of hot water, and I didn't know what I was getting into."

The few things Natalie needed upon arrival she found online. "Craigslist has been a savior here. Craigslist, Craigslist, Craigslist . . . for everything." She also always grabs the local free newspapers, since they are filled with things that are going on, and also uses a hefty Hawaii travel book, which she has found to be extremely helpful.

Natalie also suggested using Craigslist to find people who want to share shipping containers to Hawaii and split the cost.

## LIKES:

"I love jeans, big boots, and jackets. But why would you want to wear them when you want to be naked all day?" Natalie laughed, stating she loves the weather.

Natalie enjoys the surfing, too, and also likes the people; she confessed it'd be sad to move back to California. She admits she's very sensitive and enjoys the aloha from the locals, ". . . and the sunrises are so pretty." She feels that in Hawaii she can *just dwell* and live each day as it comes.

## DISLIKES:

Natalie misses the quiet ranch community she grew up in, especially the mountain air and having her own personal car. "I miss my parents horribly," she affirmed, "but my dad knows we all have a journey and he's supportive of that."

Living in such close quarters on a small island is an adjustment. Natalie revealed, "Being able to hear neighbors eat food, or have sex, or whatever they're doing," is not her ideal living situation. And, she said, after traveling for 20 minutes, you're on the other side of the island. "You can feel the edges here; you can feel the end to it."

## BEST MOMENT:

"During our first camping trip on Maui, all these little crabs would come out of the hole and one eye would pop out, and then they'd battle each other. I was laughing at them, and suddenly I looked up and watched the love of my life surfing, the bright blue water, and the white sand, and I couldn't believe I was sitting in Hawaii," Natalie reminisced.

## REGRETS:

If Natalie and Mike could have been clearer about their budget and expense account prior to relocating, it could have prevented the sudden liquidation of their savings. Also, if Mike's employer had paid for shipping all of their items, it would have saved them time, money, and aggravation upon arrival.

## ADAPTATION:

Adapting to the food choices has been difficult for Natalie and Mike. "There is an unavailability of affordable food here [compared to the mainland]. I am a healthy eater and veggies are expensive. A taco is $3.50 to $5.00 here versus $2; a bell pepper is $3.50 at Safeway; a large cucumber is $5. I found it's cheaper to go to the deli than to purchase food and eat at home."

"I feel deep in my bones that I'm here for a reason," Natalie asserted. "It's a challenge stepping away from my family who raised me. My parents are very good to me; we're very close." However Mike and Natalie have no plans to move back to the mainland. "We are pretty solidly here. This is a good place for Mike to pursue his surfboard manufacturing plans."

## BEST ADVICE:

Natalie warned that people should stop moving to Oahu because it is overcrowded and

". . . the infrastructure can't take any more people." She admitted that she shouldn't be there either. She strongly suggested the following to others pursuing relocation to Hawaii.

- Unless you have a job prior to arriving or are sure you will find full-time employment, be prepared to work two jobs to compensate for the high cost of living.

- People with breathing problems will have difficulty breathing and may get sick from the *vog* (air pollution caused by gases emitted by the erupting volcano on the Big Island).

- Understand that the plumbing, electrical, and structure of the housing will be nothing like a mainland home. You will have termites, mold, no insulation, and cock roaches.

- If you're a snob, get over it, or don't move to Hawaii unless you have a large bankroll to fund a more quality existence.

- It's absolutely necessary to have the utmost respect for the people and the land in Hawaii.

Although Natalie admitted Hawaii is beautiful, "It is very ugly; rampant with drug addicts and homeless families, and it has a cost of living that is sky rocketing due to overpopulation."

## VERDICT:

Although she loves the weather in Hawaii, Natalie admitted she has difficulty being away from her family and uses a lot of energy missing them. As long as Mike is employed, she will more than likely find herself staying in Hawaii. With her free spirit and propensity for adventure though, she may eventually relocate somewhere else entirely.

The sugar cane burning is of particular concern to Michelle; she claims it causes respiratory problems, including asthma

Michelle, Troy and their daughter
*Courtesy of Brooklynn Studios*

# CASE #22911: IT'S A GOD THING

**Perpetrator(s):** Michelle (44), Troy (41)
**Accomplice(s):** Daughter (16)
**Time in Hawaii:** 4 Years
**Island:** Maui

## BACKGROUND:

With a history of helping people while volunteering at a non-denominational Christian church in northern California, Michelle, Troy, and their young daughter were settled in their West Coast home. He provided massage services for a living, and she was content to serve in the children's ministry.

After Michelle's mother-in-law relocated to Oahu, the family took their first trip to Hawaii to visit her. When Michelle stepped off the plane in Oahu, she believed God was calling her to Hawaii. "I immediately had a deep connection to the land. That began the seeds." Later, using Oahu as a base, Michelle and Troy visited other islands. Although she liked the Big Island, she insisted, "It was too huge and desolate. It took forever to get everywhere. We felt lost. It's hard to get to the beach unless you're at a resort." It was when they arrived on Maui that Michelle felt *warm and fuzzy*. "This is where we're supposed to be."

A short time later a young pastor and his wife asked Michelle and Troy to help with the opening of a new church on Maui. Michelle knew it wasn't a coincidence. The door opened for them to start working on a move. With Troy's massage business experiencing a downturn due to the economy, and without their once thriving income, Troy and Michelle figured it wasn't going to get much better, so they made the leap to Maui sooner than later.

## FINANCES:

Although Michelle and Troy would have liked to plan better financially for their move to Maui, she admitted, "Our circumstances drove our decision." With the housing market in a slump, they were forced to sell their home for less than market value. Upon selling it, they moved into a rental property they owned. This allowed for a much lower monthly payment than they'd had previously. "We wanted to sell the house and have a nest egg. It didn't happen the way we expected," Michelle said. They arrived on Maui with about $2000.

## TRAVEL AND SHIPPING:

To earn some money for plane tickets and initial expenses on Maui, Troy and Michelle sold everything they owned except for two vehicles, two dogs, and kitchen utensils. The cars were shipped using Matson (http://matson.com/) for $1200 each and took two weeks to arrive on Maui. Michelle and her daughter left first, and one month later Troy followed with the two dogs. Their remaining boxes of pictures and other important smaller items were shipped using the U.S. Postal Service.

Of the dogs being shipped, one weighed 100 pounds and the other 11 pounds; they were shipped in the cargo area via United

Airlines for $400 and $200 respectively. Since Michelle and Troy had started the shot process for the dogs several months before leaving, they were able to avoid the quarantine process. Upon arrival, they had Central Maui Animal Clinic pick up their pets directly from the airport and clear them for direct release, which cost about $500. Overall, the cost to get each animal to Maui was a little over $1000 and included airfare, shots, and the veterinary service.

## EMPLOYMENT:

With only $2000 in their pockets, Michelle and Troy knew they'd have to find employment immediately. Since Troy was busy trying to get his massage license, he was unable to practice yet, so he secured a position quickly at Home Depot, in addition to volunteering at the new church they helped to start.

> "Unfortunately, my job is stable . . . drunk drivers keep us in business . . ."

Michelle was able to pick up a job quickly at a jewelry store in Wailea. Prior to leaving the mainland, she had applied with the Hawaii State Judiciary Department. When she arrived on Maui, she changed her address and phone number in the state's online application system and was called for an interview. This resulted in Michelle securing a job as a driver education assistant facilitating drug and alcohol classes for people who have been charged with driving under the influence, which she still holds at the time of this writing. "Unfortunately, my job is stable . . . drunk drivers keep us in business. I like the job. I don't see myself in it forever. But I am content and fortunate."

Troy began his massage service on Maui but first had to take an exam to obtain a Hawaii massage license. Unfortunately, he had to fight Hawaii's massage licensing board to take the exam because his school transcripts were no longer available, and he did not have copies since he went to school so long ago. In the end, he proved that he had worked as a massage therapist for several years in another state and was then granted the right to take the Hawaii exam. This resulted in him not having to repeat massage school, which was out of the question, Michelle said. Troy then secured an exclusive massage job at a bed and breakfast in Haiku and also gets clients by handing out business cards. In addition, he works as a landscaper with a yard maintenance company on a part-time basis and was able to quit his Home Depot position.

## HOUSING:

Prior to arriving on Maui, Michelle's mother-in-law moved from Oahu to Maui, and fortunately they were able to stay with her when they arrived on Maui. Near the time that Michelle was due to move out and find the family a new home, her mother-in-law received notice that the property she was renting was going into foreclosure. At that point, Michelle's family and Troy's mother decided to look for a house to rent together, and found one in Kihei. Finding a landlord who was willing to accept two dogs was much more difficult than they had anticipated.

After living in the Kihei house for one year, Michelle and Troy's lease was up. Troy's mother wanted to have her own home again, so Michelle and Troy were on their own in their house hunting. At that time a realtor friend from their church told them about a friend's little historic house in Wailuku that had been vacated because it was going into foreclosure. The realtor offered to let the family stay there free of charge until the bank arrived to take possession. Michelle and Troy jumped at the chance to have somewhere to live free of charge but admitted, "It was built in 1937. There were termites holding it together." But they moved in anyway. Six months later, the bank did knock on their door and said they had to pay rent. The bank agreed upon a mere $700 per month, which was significantly below market value. Two years later Michelle and Troy received a sold notice from the bank and were given 45 days to move out.

Michelle and Troy found a two-bedroom ohana in Kahului, and the landlord accepted dogs. It was a bit small for them, but they were thankful at least to have somewhere to live. Near the end of their lease period, Michelle confirmed that what happened next was *a God thing*. Their realtor friend again told them about a Kihei property. It involved assuming responsibility for the existing lease of a tenant who had to vacate the property. Michelle and Troy told the realtor that they were not in need of a new place to live because they were under the assumption that they would be signing another lease for their current rental. To Michelle and Troy's surprise, the next day they received another notice to vacate! The owners of their current rental decided to move back into the property, forcing Michelle and Troy to move again.

Luckily, Michelle and Troy had a housing option that had been offered to them just the previous day! One quick call secured that rental for them. Although they feel blessed to have housing for their family in Maui's sparse rental market, they are not fond of Kihei because of the air quality.

> Although they feel blessed to have housing for their family in Maui's sparse rental market, they are not fond of Kihei because of the air quality.

"Kihei is surrounded by sugarcane fields. It produces ash and poor air; it's super windy all the time during the [burning] season, which is typically from March to December." Michelle wishes she could keep her windows open; however because of the sugarcane, there is a *horrible* smell that blows into Kihei. According to Michelle, burning is the easiest way for the cane to be harvested.

Michelle has some favorite parts of Maui that she would love to live in. "I loved Wailuku. There's so much opportunity to love on people," or minister to others. She also enjoys the cooler, breezier, and more temperate climate of the upcountry's Pukalani, Makawao, and lower Kula.

Upcountry Maui

The beach becomes part of many events and activities, including family pictures! *Courtesy of Brooklynn Studios*

## SCHOOLING:

When Michelle and Troy arrived on Maui, their daughter was in middle school. She now attends Maui High in Kahului. "She used to get hassled . . . a lot . . . when she started. Name calling . . . cyber bullying . . . rumors. But now since she's staying [on Maui], she is left alone."

Michelle claims that the relationships her daughter has formed are very shallow, unlike the deep friendships she had on the mainland. "There are lots of drug-and-alcohol-based relationships. And she doesn't do that." Michelle shared a recent survey she read that showed 50 percent of Maui kids use alcohol.

Michelle and Troy's daughter is *dying to leave* the island to go to college, and her parents wish she was having a better experience. "School is challenging. She used to love school; now she just tolerates it."

## ACTIVITIES:

Between work and church, Michelle and Troy don't get to enjoy the outdoors as often as they'd like. She loves going beachcombing and has tried surfing but has taken more to paddle boarding and just walking to enjoy the weather. Her daughter plays sports through school, including track and swimming. Troy golfs often at Waiehu Golf Course near Wailuku, and with a local ID, the cost is only $10 a game. Michelle did go on a spur-of-the-moment hike in Iao Valley in Wailuku, but she really doesn't take advantage of the hiking trails Maui has to offer.

## SOCIALIZATION AND INTEGRATION:

When Troy and Michelle were originally compelled to move to Hawaii, it was because help was needed with the planning of a new church. Although that church still exists, Troy and Michelle met another couple who shared a similar vision, and they now co-pastor a home fellowship called The Journey Maui. They still keep in touch with the first couple, but now most of their friendships are developed through their home-based church in Kihei.

## HELPFUL RESOURCES:

The Hawaii state employment website was where Michelle submitted her job application online (http://dhrd.hawaii.gov/job-seekers/). As a reminder, Michelle stressed the importance of having an 808 phone number; if not, then ". . . they are not interested in you."

Michelle also looked for jobs through these two websites (http://www.indeed.com/ and http://www.monster.com/) and Craigslist. She also scanned the *Maui News* newspaper when it was free to search for jobs, but Michelle states they charge a fee now to search.

Troy registered for his Hawaii massage license exam by visiting the state website (http://hawaii.gov/dcaa/pvl/boards/massage/).

More information can be found about the sugar cane burning at http://hcsugar.com/.

## LIKES:

The thing Michelle likes most about Hawaii is the weather. "I am a warm weather person. I don't need all of the seasons. But sometimes I miss it. I have seasonal affective disorder, and I would get depressed and stay that way for a long time." Maui helps to combat that in Michelle.

Michelle truly loves the culture of Hawaii, but she has noticed it's disappearing. "It's barely hanging on . . . it's so commercialized you have to dig for it. You're not gonna find it at a luau . . . you're not gonna find it at a gallery. We're never going to get it unless we look for it."

Michelle admits that Hawaii is a beautiful place with a light and dark side to it. "There's a lot of dark and there's light peering in and we're clinging to it." She and her family try to enjoy the beauty of Hawaii by connecting with nature whenever possible.

## DISLIKES:

Michelle confesses that drivers on Maui . . . tourists and locals alike, do not drive with aloha. She worries about the dangerous situations that drivers cause. "Every single day we have to fight traffic and poor driving."

The sugar cane burning is of particular concern to Michelle; she claims it causes respiratory problems, including asthma. "The whole sugar cane debate is a hot button [and a] sensitive topic on the island." The smell and fumes affect many parts of the island, she added. "If you live in Kahului and anywhere near the mill, it can blanket the entire area in a stench that is not easily explained. Frankly, it smells like a cross between a portable toilet, spoiled cheese, and bad Mexican food." Michelle understands, however, that the mill supports many families, and the locals are used to the effects of the burning.

The high expense is *right up there* on Michelle's list of Maui dislikes. "There's a lack of affordable housing. I worry every time our lease comes up for renewal. God tells us not to worry, but I still find myself worrying about it. It's very difficult."

## BEST MOMENT:

When Michelle stepped off the plane in Oahu during her first visit, she knew she was destined to be in Hawaii. Regardless of the hardships and uncertainty she and her family have faced, Michelle refocuses herself on God's majesty as she's watching a sunset, or when she sees another life saved [by God], or when she watches the rain fall on the mountains, or when she connects with others on a deep level. "It's about having community."

## REGRETS:

Michelle wishes she had spent more time researching the island prior to arriving. She could have been more educated about the different parts of it and learned more about housing so she would have been prepared for the lack of available housing with pets. Saving more money would have definitely eased some of the obstacles she and her family have experienced.

## ADAPTATION:

Michelle reminisced about their first few weeks on Maui when they were newcomers. "Ironically, it was very hard to move. It didn't feel real, more like we were on vacation. I found myself getting very fearful very quickly. *Did we make a mistake? Did we make the right decision? Did we hear God correctly?* I cried every moment my daughter went to middle school. But we as Christians are called to walk in faith, not necessarily seeking peace and contentment." Adapting to life on Maui has been a process for Michelle and her family.

Michelle and her family have come a long way since they arrived. "I'd like to think I'm still earning aloha," Michelle said. She tries to slow down and not rush with people. She believes she must give in order to receive but never expects anything in return. "It's an ongoing process . . . to be comfortable in the community. It's a process of trust."

Michelle was surprised after a recent trip to Ohio to visit her parents. "I went back for the first time . . . it was a strange experience . . . I felt different . . . I was thankful to go back [to Maui]."

## BEST ADVICE:

Michelle wants others to know that Hawaii is suffering. "The land has been hurting for some time. People who go to Maui with a lack of a spiritual connection end up *getting spit out.* They leave scorched land and people continue the cycle. They should have a lot more thought going into [moving]."

Listed below are some important points Michelle thinks others should consider prior to moving to Hawaii.

+ Research jobs prior to leaving the mainland.

+ Know the culture of where you're going.

+ Check out Hawaiian history . . . the state didn't come easy.

+ Know that you have to earn aloha in Hawaii.

+ Give more than you receive.

+ Be open.

+ Look for opportunities to help others.

+ Ask questions.

Lastly, she added, "Always smile . . . you don't have to talk . . . not everyone wants to strike up a conversation."

## VERDICT:

Michelle said she and her family will stay on Maui until God calls them elsewhere. "There's no other place in my heart that I'm drawn to. We will even deal with the housing problems . . . but we still look at homes for sale so we can have a church that everyone knows and can count on."

Alice volunteers her time to conservation efforts at the Kilauea Lighthouse

Alice and Cecil enjoying a day at the beach

# CASE #19555: RETIRED AND READY

**Perpetrator(s):** Alice (61), Cecil (65)
**Accomplice(s):** None
**Time In Hawaii:** 3.5 Years
**Island:** Kauai

## BACKGROUND:

After vacationing in Hawaii for many years, Alice and Cecil decided to spend extended time on the island of Kauai. That first year they stayed a month, the next three months, and the next six months. It was during that last six-month trip that Cecil urged Alice to take the leap with him and purchase property on the North Shore. This came as a surprise to Alice since they'd had no plans to move to Hawaii any time in the near future. Cecil started looking at real estate, and ". . . he got crazy about moving," Alice said.

Alice remained hesitant to relocate because of the life she was leaving behind. Though she was already retired from her 30-year emergency dispatch career, she and Cecil had nieces and nephews they were very close to and even considered them as their own children, not to mention their mother, Alice's sister. Alice had never wandered from her hometown in Washington State. She and Cecil's five-acre hobby farm (a small farm operated for pleasure rather than for income) had been home to them for years.

Alice realized that the move was something Cecil had to do. She and Cecil, along with his handyman skills that he had honed as a homebuilder, took the leap of faith to Kauai.

## FINANCES:

Since Cecil and Alice were already retired, there was no financial planning involved in orchestrating a move to Hawaii. Alice was skeptical about drawing money from their nest egg that was supposed to go toward traveling during their retirement years; however it was necessary in order to place a down payment on a house. Cecil promised that she wouldn't have to worry about money and that he would make it work by earning income on the island. They still do intend on traveling but will wait until two pieces of real estate in Washington sell in order to reimburse their travel fund.

## TRAVEL AND SHIPPING:

Prior to leaving Washington, Alice and Cecil had a two-day estate sale that was *huge;* the items for sale filled a three-stall garage and most of the inside of the house. Although they filled a 20-foot container with their belongings to be shipped by Matson (http://www.matson.com/), they sold a lot of what they owned including *tons and tons of farm stuff.* "We just cleaned house," Alice recalled. She was surprised that about one-third of the Matson container was filled with tools and other items that would be necessary for Cecil to complete handyman jobs on Kauai.

Alice was impressed with Matson. "They came in and packed everything . . . they packed good. They know what they're doing. There wasn't one thing broken."

Cecil and Alice left some important things with her sister, like art and other heirlooms. However, Alice was sure to take her dining room table ". . . because that's where everyone gathered through the years so it has sentimental value."

## EMPLOYMENT:

Cecil followed through on his promise to earn income by working as a handyman. He placed ads on Craigslist, and that resulted in obtaining a very good and consistent job at a 100-year-old estate that needed continual repairs and upkeep on the North Shore. He also answered additional job ads placed on Craigslist, and Alice and Cecil's real estate agent continues to be a good source of referrals.

## HOUSING:

Two months before they were scheduled to finish their six-month Kauai vacation, Alice and Cecil purchased a home on the North Shore in Princeville, and it closed during the last month of their vacation. They chose the North Shore because they are both into nature, and the beauty is *outstanding* on the North Shore. They also love that there are *not nearly as many people* there as in other parts of the island. "It's more country . . . more our style. There are no spotlights . . . it's a small town feel."

After purchasing the Princeville house and immediately prior to leaving the island, Alice and Cecil purchased a vehicle and left it at their new home. They also rented out their new house through Home Exchange until they were able to return to Kauai.

Three months after they left their Kauai vacation, Alice and Cecil returned to the island using one-way tickets. When they arrived to their new home, they went straight to their empty house. The

Cecil enjoying the sunset from the lanai at the St. Regis Princeville on Kauai.

container with their furniture arrived a few days later, followed by their vehicle several days after that.

Alice admitted that the first year in Kauai was *crazy*. She and Cecil flew back and forth to Washington a few times in order to facilitate the sale of some of their property. This, of course, could have been avoided if they hadn't moved so quickly.

Since settling in Princeville, Alice has found that she loves it very much. She said the neighbors are wonderful but warns newcomers that most people keep their windows open, which allows everyone to hear each other's business. Princeville has closer quarters than Alice and Cecil experienced when living on their five-acre farm, with houses in Princeville that are about 25 feet away from each other. They do enjoy the potlucks once a month and also watching the children ride their bikes on the cul-de-sac.

Alice calls Princeville a "haole community" and noted that there are both retired people as well as families who make Princeville their home.

## SCHOOLING:

N/A

## ACTIVITIES:

Alice loves the 80-degree water temperature. She is outdoors every day walking Hanalei Bay or biking on the Princeville paths. "The scenery is just gorgeous . . . you just want to be outside." Her favorite snorkeling spots are Tunnels Beach and Ke'e Beach and for swimming, Lumahai Beach. In the winter she and Cecil frequent Anini Beach because the big reef provides protection from the rough water.

Hiking is not the first thing on Alice's list when it comes to activities. "The trails are real slippery and not very user friendly." She has hiked the Sleeping Giant trail and admitted it was a challenge. "It was gorgeous . . . worth dragging yourself up for the view."

Cecil and Alice often golf at Wailua Municipal Golf Course, a public course located in Lihue. She said, "It is well maintained, with several signature holes along the ocean. It's one of the best in the islands." A person under 65 years old can golf for only $60 per month; if over 65, the cost is $40 per month, not including the golf cart.

The movie theater, Kukuhi Grove Cinemas, has recently undergone a renovation and is now *very safe* compared to its previous condition, Alice said. She tries to go to the movies at least a couple times a month.

The bamboo bridge at McBryde Garden, a National Tropical Botannical Garden, on Kauai

## SOCIALIZATION AND INTEGRATION:

Alice meets others through volunteering at the Kilauea Lighthouse, while Cecil meets people through his work. They have also found it easy to meet others when attending other activities. When Cecil and Alice went to the National Tropical Botanical Gardens in Koloa, they made a connection with another retired couple that they still see occasionally, and they are now starting to meet new neighbors and share the relocation experience in common with them. "You need people connections to feel like you belong. I needed to establish myself here. I needed a friend," Alice confessed.

## HELPFUL RESOURCES:

Cecil has used Craigslist to obtain jobs throughout the island. He and Alice use the island's stores to purchase everything they need. Every two weeks they make the 45-minute drive to Lihue, making stops at Costco, Home Depot, a gas station, and Longs Drugs. They find that everything they need is available on the island.

Cecil and Alice found real estate agent Jill Smith of Resort Properties of the Pacific at an open house they visited during their last vacation on Kauai. "We were very happy with her," Alice said.

## LIKES:

One of the reasons Cecil and Alice love Kauai is because of its North Shore. "The rain doesn't stop you like it does when you're on vacation. I need rain. I like it. Rain is not a deal breaker," Alice shared.

Kauai's laid-back approach to life is something Cecil and Alice relish. "The pace is slower here. It's a simpler life since there are not all the distractions like amusement parks or large shopping malls or big sporting events to rush off to," she said.

It is also easier to have a healthy lifestyle, Alice acknowledged. "There is an abundance of fresh food, and with the sunshine and breezes to cool you, you want to be active and outdoors because it feels so good."

Cecil and Alice

Cecil and Alice also enjoy the small size of the island and consider the residents warm and welcoming. "People smile more, take time to talk and even let you in when there is a line of traffic. It is truly easier to find and experience the sense of what they call aloha here," she shared.

## DISLIKES:

The warm year-round weather has its downside, Alice confesses. "For this Northwest girl, it can get too hot and humid for me in the summer months. Even though the temperature only fluctuates a few degrees, from 78 to 86, the real feel can be in the 90s in the summer with usually added humidity."

The medical system is something Alice and Cecil will have to adjust to. Kauai does not currently have a medical facility that accepts their insurance, so they are in essence without medical coverage on the island, and a medical procedure such as a colonoscopy or endoscopy can only be provided by traveling to Oahu, Alice confirmed. However, emergency procedures are covered by her and Cecil's insurance on Kauai, and there are emergency facilities on the island.

Thoughtfully reflecting on being away from family, Alice considered the consequences of moving. "It is a long way from family and life-long friends. It was tough and lonely at times to leave behind so many people and pets I loved. Not having the frequent contact I was used to is definitely the hardest part about being here."

Though Alice is thankful there are no snakes on Kauai, she considers centipedes the closest comparison. "We spray every three months with bug killer (Ortho). It also takes care of the cockroaches and ants." No centipedes have been seen in the house and when one is seen in the garage, it is either dead or dying from the spray. "We are careful where we put our hands when working outside, and I always shake out my gloves before I put them on."

## BEST MOMENT:

About three years after Alice and Cecil's relocation to Kauai, she had an epiphany that turned out to be just what she needed. Struggling to find pure happiness on Kauai, Alice decided to extend a summer trip to Washington for a few extra months. Those extra few months proved to her that she didn't have to choose between Washington and Hawaii. She could have both. "I no longer felt like either/or; the four months showed me that wasn't the case." She was able to phase out of her old home and phase into her new one. "Washington is my heart home . . . but Hawaii is my physical home and is becoming more my home the longer I'm here."

> "Washington is my heart home . . . but Hawaii is my physical home and is becoming more my home the longer I'm here."

Upon returning to Kauai after that trip, she felt more of a sense of contentment. Although they travel together to Washington, Alice stays in Washington a few extra months while Cecil goes back to work on Kauai because he doesn't need that extra time in Washington to adjust to his new Kauai life.

## REGRETS:

Though Cecil and Alice's full-time relocation to Kauai was unplanned, they don't regret having gone through the obstacles they encountered. The new adventure, although filled with *trepidation and uncertainty*, was a welcome change in their lives. "I can't imagine missing this experience. I feel very lucky," Alice shared.

## ADAPTATION:

Each summer now Alice stays in Washington, which has helped her adapt more easily to Kauai. "We definitely feel like islanders

now. The slower pace, Aloha Spirit, outdoors, and community lifestyle is who we are now."

Cecil and Alice have integrated in and accepted the Kauai culture. Alice explained, "We have embraced the goodness found here in the culture and lifestyle of ohana, aloha, and *kuleana* (right, privilege, and responsibility) for this *aina* (earth or land)."

Alice throwing a *shaka* (a hand gesture meaning *hang loose*) that is part of the Aloha Spirit she enjoys

## BEST ADVICE:

Alice offers advice, listed below, to others hoping to relocate to Hawaii.

- ◆ Do your homework.

- ◆ Spend time in Hawaii, months if you can, to see if island life is what you expected it to be.

- ◆ Look hard at the numbers, because everything is imported, so it is expensive compared to the mainland.

- Really think about what you will be leaving behind . . . the people, activities, and places.

- List the pros and cons of relocating.

- Research each island because they each have different things to offer.

## VERDICT:

Cecil and Alice believe they will stay on the island and have no future plans to move back to Washington. "This is our life now. This is where we live. I have found my balance with my old life and my new life with summers planned in the Northwest with family and friends. I am happy . . . and very blessed," Alice said optimistically.

Alice and Cecil enjoying the Quiksilver Eddie Aikau Big Wave Competition on the North Shore

The view from the Diamond Head Trail that Janelle said ". . . has great views and [is] a pretty easy hike."

Janelle and Rod

## CASE #36729: GIRL MEETS BOY

**Perpetrator(s):** Janelle (33), Rod (33)
**Accomplice(s):** None
**Time In Hawaii:** 7 Months
**Island:** Oahu

### BACKGROUND:

Growing up in California and then moving to Arizona with her family after high school, Janelle had her share of new experiences. From sales to bookkeeping, she stayed busy until she graduated from college with a degree in global and business financial management. With an aptitude for numbers, she secured an accounting job in Phoenix after graduation.

Janelle was no stranger to Hawaii. She had visited Maui, Oahu, and Lanai in the past, and had always considered relocating to the islands. "I thought of moving to Hawaii in previous years. I looked at jobs available and figured *I can pull it off.*" But she was always hesitant to take the leap. Later when she saw a posting on Facebook that mentioned *something about house sitting on Oahu*, she responded to the posting. "It took a long time for someone to call me back," she said. When they did call back, Janelle learned that a friend of a friend needed a house and pet sitter on Oahu for a month. It didn't take long for Janelle to decide to take the temporary job. She bought a one-way ticket, and within three weeks she was on Oahu.

## FINANCES:

Unlike a lot of people, Janelle's strong suit was saving money. "I am good with money. I always had a savings." Building her accounting clientele, she was able to maintain a savings account so purchasing a ticket to Hawaii didn't significantly impact her finances.

> "We mainly eat salads at home so we can eat the unhealthy stuff when we go out . . ."

Janelle has found a way to keep costs down in Hawaii; she eats at home most of the time due to the high food prices. "We mainly eat salads at home so we can eat the unhealthy stuff when we go out. Target has good prices on groceries, believe it or not."

## TRAVEL AND SHIPPING:

Since Janelle was only going to Oahu for a month, she didn't worry about long-term plans. She packed one carry-on bag with enough to get her through a month. The house-sitting position also provided Janelle with a vehicle so she didn't have to rent one upon arrival. Her vehicle in Arizona was stored at her grandparents' house until she returned home the following month.

Since Janelle stayed on Oahu when her house-sitting position was completed, her parents shipped her vehicle for her through Matson (http://www.matson.com/), and this cost about $1100. She got by without a vehicle until it arrived because she provided accounting services to her mainland clients from her Oahu home; therefore no car travel was required.

## EMPLOYMENT:

The owner of the house where Janelle would be house sitting over-nighted the car keys to Janelle before she left the mainland. When she arrived on Oahu, she was faced with the arduous task of locating the vehicle in the airport parking lot, not knowing where it was or what it looked like. After successfully finding the car, Janelle was able to drive directly to the house in Honolulu because she had the address. After three weeks and one day, her house- and pet-sitting job was finished.

When Janelle decided to make Oahu a more permanent home, she struggled with how she was going to maintain her mainland clients. She assured them that she could still perform her job from a distance, and at the same time, she started networking on Oahu for new clients. She joined BNI Networking Group (http://www .bnihawaii.com/) and began getting referrals. In addition, through Facebook, Janelle found a part-time seasonal accounting position in Downtown Honolulu preparing yearly tax returns.

## HOUSING:

During the time that Janelle was house and pet sitting, she met Rod, a Coast Guard employee, through a dating website titled Plenty of Fish (http://www.pof.com/). When her house-sitting obligation was completed, she and Rod were still dating. She wasn't ready to leave the island yet, so Rod found temporary housing for her on the island so she could stay three more weeks. After realizing that the housing option Rod found was too far from his home, making it inconvenient to see each other, they decided she would move in with him for her remaining weeks on Oahu.

Janelle and Rod made a list of sights to see before Janelle left. One month and a lot of tourist attractions later, she wanted to stay and he wanted her to stay, so she started to make arrangements to end her existing apartment lease in Arizona and establish permanent residency on Oahu. Luckily, Janelle was in a good position to wrap

Janelle's view while working from home

things up at her old apartment. "I'd already condensed my things [prior to the Oahu trip] because I wanted to move somewhere." Her family cleaned out Janelle's apartment; her sister stored some of her things and is using others until Janelle needs them. The only things left were Janelle's clothes, and the family shipped them to her.

## SCHOOLING:

Although never an instructor, Janelle has practiced yoga and is looking into obtaining yoga certification on Oahu. However, she can only find a month-long course, and she needs a shorter one.

## ACTIVITIES:

Janelle frequents Sunset Beach for *chilling* and likes Bellows Beach for swimming and boogie boarding. She enjoys yoga on her patio and running through her Ewa Beach neighborhood. She used to enjoy running to Sandy Beach Park in Honolulu while she was house sitting. She has hiked the Diamond Head trail and said it ". . . has great views and [is] a pretty easy hike." She noticed that she's outside much more on Oahu than she was in California or Arizona.

Janelle and Rod enjoy many happy hours together at Rum Fire; it's on the beach and has some fun drinks. They also like Real Gastro Pub because it has a lot of different craft beers on tap. The Monkey Pod is also enjoyable and offers live music and good food.

Rod and Janelle even went to Greece and Germany for the Oktoberfest. "Most people think [when they live here] they're on vacation, so they don't go on vacation." This, however, is not true for Janelle. Only five months into her Oahu residency, Janelle went back to Arizona for her niece's birthday celebration.

## SOCIALIZATION AND INTEGRATION:

Since meeting Rod online, Janelle hasn't had to make any efforts to meet others, because she meets many people through Rod, since he grew up on the island. One of Janelle's brother's friends lives on Oahu, and she was able to get together with and meet others through her. Janelle has befriended the owner of the house where she had the house-sitting job and has get-togethers periodically with her.

Janelle is doing her best to learn Hawaiian words but still can't pronounce them properly. "People throw in Hawaiian language when talking," which Janelle said makes it difficult to understand what they're saying. She has also visited many cultural sights and events including the Bon Dance, a yearly festival held at Japanese temples throughout the islands.

## HELPFUL RESOURCES:

Janelle used Facebook quite a bit at the beginning of her stay on Oahu to find housing, but with Rod to help her, she doesn't need any other resources to find her way.

## LIKES:

Janelle's quick answer to what she likes about Oahu: "Rod!" But that's not all. "The weather's amazing . . . not hot. I'm just outside a lot. [I like] the beaches of course. The palmyra trees . . . the palm trees . . . the rainbows . . . the views . . . and the people are nice."

Janelle adapting to the Hawaiian culture at Waimanalo Beach

Janelle likes the Hawaiian lifestyle where people are *not showy*. "They don't have fancy stuff . . . it's not the focus for people in Hawaii. Hawaii fits my lifestyle, too."

## DISLIKES:

As soon as Janelle got on the highway from the airport and drove to her new house-sitting residence, she noticed the traffic. "The Oahu freeway is really crazy . . . it sucks!" She was amazed that it took two hours to go 20 miles. "But it's just when you're going downtown . . . from 8 a.m. to 2 p.m. traffic is cool . . . most of the time." She noted that the drivers are *all right*. "Most people have a Hawaiian attitude . . . the Aloha Spirit."

Janelle is still getting used to the expense of groceries and housing. "Groceries are insane!" She claims that her and Rod's *super-teeny* one-bedroom apartment is a great deal at $1100 per month. "It's not the nicest place."

## BEST MOMENT:

The most defining moment for Janelle was when she had not yet committed to staying on Oahu. She and Rod were planning a trip to Greece, and the plan was for Janelle to fly back to Arizona from

Greece while Rod flew back to Oahu. It was at that moment that she decided she wanted to fly back to Oahu with Rod. "I called my parents right away to liquidate my belongings and send my car."

## REGRETS:

"It would have been nice to be more organized . . . have movers move my stuff instead of family. It was hard for them."

## ADAPTATION:

Janelle believes she is fitting in with the Hawaiian lifestyle and takes advantage of the slower pace. She and Rod go to the beach often just to have a drink and relax.

## BEST ADVICE:

Janelle offered a few simple pieces of advice listed below for those who are thinking about taking the leap to Hawaii.

- ◆ Network with others in business and personally.

- ◆ Ask people who, where, what . . . to go, to do, etc.

- ◆ You have to LOVE it to stay, but if you love Hawaii, you love it; bugs or other little things that may bother you elsewhere won't bother you here.

## VERDICT:

The length of Janelle's stay on Oahu will be based on Rod's future with the Coast Guard. "We will stay as long as we can. I love Hawaii, but I love Rod more. We will be a little reluctant to leave but we'll be back. If we don't live here full time [again], we will be here a lot."

Ethan enjoys hiking in the Waipio Valley and
". . . picks fresh fruit off of the tons of fruit trees."

Ethan performing

# CASE #42122: FINDING EDEN

**Perpetrator(s):** Ethan (30)
**Accomplice(s):** None
**Time In Hawaii:** 2 Years
**Island:** Big Island

## BACKGROUND:

Reading books about Hawaii wasn't enough for Ethan, an organic vegan food cart owner in Portland, Oregon. Practicing healthy and sustainable living as close as one can in a rainy, wet, and cold environment, Ethan had a desire to grow his own food and live off the land. After a house fire that displaced him, Ethan began his search for inner peace that surprisingly came through *Ho'oponopono*, an ancient Hawaiian practice of reconciliation and forgiveness that invited him to live in harmony with nature.

Obtaining his massage therapist license in Oregon after the fire, the wisdom Ethan gained through his readings about Hawaii prompted him to learn Hawaiian massage. He took a trip to Maui to attend the Tandem Sacred Temple *Lomilomi* (meaning to knead or rub), a weekend-long Hawaiian massage course. It was during that Maui trip that he had an epiphany. "On the road to Hana, I was so overwhelmed with the energy of the island that I broke down in tears. I knew then that my future was in Hawaii."

With an even deeper desire to jump full force into organic farming, Ethan researched and found a Big Island organic farmer who needed help. Within 30 days, he was on a one-way flight to a Hilo farm on the Big Island.

## FINANCES:

It didn't cross Ethan's mind to save money. He knew he'd have free lodging and food at his volunteer farming position. What he didn't plan for was when his time at the farm would conclude. He admitted, "I should have planned better." However, Ethan is able to save money now because of his creativity in generating income in a variety of ways.

## TRAVEL AND SHIPPING:

A one-way ticket on Hawaiian Airlines to the Big Island was all it took for Ethan to relocate to Hawaii, along with a bike, suitcase, and guitar. He flew from Portland to Hilo, which has a much smaller airport than Kona and offers more limited flights compared to Kona. Ethan had biked in Portland and was planning on biking in his new home.

## EMPLOYMENT:

When he arrived on the Big Island, Ethan volunteered at an organic farm near Hilo. He found this farm through the Worldwide Opportunities on Organic Farms (http://www.wwoof.net/), an organization that links volunteers with organic farms and growers. These are not paid jobs; however a volunteer receives housing, food, or both (as in Ethan's case), in exchange for labor. This initial position allowed Ethan the opportunity to settle into island life without having to worry about food, housing, or a job. (Although technically the organic farm wasn't employment, Ethan stayed on for only a month due to a falling out with the farm owner.)

After a few months of moving around the island to pursue free housing options, Ethan finally obtained employment. "It never occurred to me until then that I needed a job! The level of consciousness is different [here], because love and food is in abundance. You don't need money to be happy." He was open to any type of work and accepted a position mopping the floors at a health food store. It was while mopping floors that Ethan determined he would ". . . do whatever it takes to stay on the island."

> ". . . The level of consciousness is different [here], because love and food is in abundance. You don't need money to be happy."

The mopping job didn't last long; he was found drinking kava on the job. Even though Ethan maintained that kava is legal and was sold in the store he was working at, he was fired because it is considered to be a controlled substance. He did not know this. Soon after, another health food store hired him and this proved to be the most difficult and demanding job Ethan had ever had. "I was never made to feel so low class in my life. I was treated so poorly by the other workers; it was inhumane treatment." Consequently he quit that job and admitted, "I felt lost. I didn't plan." Ethan then decided to obtain his Hawaii massage license.

Ethan is now a massage therapist at a clinic in Hilo. He also rents out rooms and offers yoga and breakfast to visitors in his four-bedroom Hilo home through the website (http://www.booking.com) under the name 360 Yoga Bed and Breakfast, which contributes significantly to Ethan's income. He also works part-time leasing bamboo vending spaces in Hilo for the private owner. Ethan admitted that although he would have liked to continue his food cart business that he operated in Portland, he doesn't think it's a viable career on the Big Island because of the high costs of parking a cart.

Ethan is also starting a distribution company called Hawaiian Health Paradigm that will deliver high quality indigenous and local products to grocers on the U.S. East and West Coasts.

## HOUSING:

After Ethan left the farm, he was fortunate to secure free room and board with a friend and her parents in Kona. After two months, he followed that same friend to Hilo and lived with her for two months. When she moved back to Kona, it was the first time Ethan was faced with having to find a place to stay where he had to pay rent. He rented a *shed* in Hilo, and by a shed, he meant a shed! "It had four walls, a window, and a door. I used the bathroom in the main house." After a month in the shed, Ethan decided to rent a house in Hilo where he could sublet bedrooms to vacationers for short periods.

In the future, Ethan is planning on living *off-grid* (not connected to a main power or water source) to pursue his dream of living a self-sustaining life on the Big Island.

## SCHOOLING:

Ethan only had to take a Hawaii state exam for his massage license since he had already completed school on the mainland. "I showed up to a room at a church-type of place," he remembered, and took the test for $150.

## ACTIVITIES:

Ethan's main focus has been playing his bass guitar with hopes of making it his career. He also focuses on farming and on offering massage services. Although he took his guitar to the Big Island, he wasn't much of a player until after he arrived. Now involved in four different bands, Ethan has played in over 50 shows, or gigs, throughout the past year.

In addition to Ethan's busy music and massage schedule, he still finds time to visit the beach and to go hiking. One of his favorite beaches is Black Sand Beach in Waipio

Ethan performing

Valley. According to Ethan, it's not so great for swimming but good for surfing and camping, which Ethan has yet to try. "There are a river and waterfalls, with horse boarding . . . and recluses!" He also hikes in that area and ". . . picks fresh fruit off of the tons of fruit trees."

## SOCIALIZATION AND INTEGRATION:

Five months after Ethan moved to the Big Island, his girlfriend followed, so during those first few months he didn't socialize with others much. However, Ethan finds he socializes more now that he and his girlfriend have parted ways. He plays music often at the Bayfront Kava Bar, which doesn't serve alcohol but serves kava, the traditional Polynesian drink that *relaxes and soothes*. Ethan meets others easily there and met his current girlfriend at another club where he was playing.

## HELPFUL RESOURCES:

As mentioned, Ethan found his organic farming opportunity through Worldwide Opportunities on Organic Farms (http://www.wwoof .net/), an organization that connects volunteers with farmers.

Ethan used Craigslist to find his current rental, but he doesn't find a need for it otherwise.

The State of Hawaii Department of Commerce and Consumer Affairs is the organization that handles the massage licensing. The application forms can be found at http://hawaii.gov/dcca/pvl/boards/ massage/.

## LIKES:

With Ethan's history and his attraction to a self-sustaining lifestyle, it is not surprising that the Big Island's ecosystem is his favorite thing about the island. "It's a paradise for people who can see it. An intact isolated living ecosystem is as close to Eden as I can identify."

## DISLIKES:

Ethan's connection to the Big Island has led to his support of its independence. "[Hawaii] is under illegal U.S. military occupation. The kingdom of Hawaii was never lawfully annexed into U.S. juris-diction. It was taken by force from the Queen by gunpoint. And it's never since been dissolved." The U.S. government's drone training around the Hawaiian Islands also frustrates him, he said.

## BEST MOMENT:

Ethan's friend, who traveled on a transcontinental bike ride from the southernmost point of Florida to the northernmost point of Alaska, was the one who supported his move to Hawaii. "He convinced me that anything is possible." Ethan said that solidified his move.

## REGRETS:

The only regret Ethan can conjure up involves his past relationship. "I would have broken up with my ex-girlfriend before flying her here and unconsciously paying her way."

## ADAPTATION:

Not only does Ethan connect to the land, he also relates well to the residents of the island and has adopted the island's way of life. "The mentality of people here is to take care of this Eden. Respect to the land is self-respect. We do not see ourselves as separate from the aina. We are *kama'aina*, which translates to people of the land. It is a mindset. I adopted it when I got here and have been cherishing the fruits of its belief."

## BEST ADVICE:

The connection Ethan has to the land is reflected in his one piece of advice to others: "Your life wants you to trust it."

## VERDICT:

For Ethan, living in Hawaii is not permanent even though he admitted, "Hawaii is my home. I never felt more at home anywhere else. I will travel around the world serving the highest good. With that intention I will perform my music, make art, bring healing work wherever I go, engage in

Ethan lying in a garden of roses

local lifestyles and cultures, and get to know myself on the deepest of all levels."

Kelly reminisced, "The rainbows . . .
I love them and miss seeing them
after the rains."

Kelly, Tony and their children at White Plains Beach

# CASE #32041: UNEXPECTED

**Perpetrator(s):** Kelly (42), Tony (46)
**Accomplice(s):** Daughter (10), Son (7),
Daughter (19 Months)
**Time In Hawaii:** 3.5 Years
**Island:** Oahu

## BACKGROUND:

Growing up the daughter of a missionary and living in Ecuador while her father taught missionary children, Kelly learned to adapt to another culture when she was young. However, when her husband Tony announced they were moving to Oahu because his auto rental company was transferring him, Kelly had mixed feelings. "I felt angry. I didn't want to leave Nevada. We had just moved there nine months before Tony was offered the position in Hawaii."

At the time of Tony's announcement, Kelly didn't draw on her Ecuadorian experiences. "I really did not think about it. I just saw my move to Hawaii as moving to another state. We were going there for my husband's job. It wasn't until I moved to Hawaii and started living there that I realized all the cultural issues."

Kelly anxiously considered the possible hardships of moving a family with two children across the ocean. The family had been transferred to Reno, Nevada, just nine months before the new Hawaii transfer opportunity was presented to them; however the reality was that Tony would not have a job if they didn't move. He and Kelly realized that living in Hawaii with a job was better than living in Nevada without one. Within a few weeks, Tony was on a plane to Oahu to start his new position.

Kelly stayed in Reno with the two children until the house sold. Luckily for her and Tony, they knew his auto rental company would purchase their house in Reno if it didn't sell on its own. Unfortunately, that was exactly what Kelly had to wait for.

Four months after Tony left, the rest of the family joined him for an adventure that would abruptly conclude in a move off the island three and a half years later.

## FINANCES:

Kelly and Tony did not have to worry about finances or take time to plan the move to Hawaii. His employer covered all of the costs associated with the move, and since Tony was already employed prior to leaving, there was no stress about securing an income source.

## TRAVEL AND SHIPPING:

Tony and Kelly used United Van Lines Horizon Moving Systems to ship all of their household belongings in a container, including one vehicle. Tony's employer scheduled and paid for the move, thereby relieving Kelly and him of the task.

## EMPLOYMENT:

By the time Kelly arrived on Oahu with the kids, Tony was already working at the auto rental company. She was apprehensive about the move to Oahu but was excited about Tony's substantial salary increase. However, her excitement soon diminished when she discovered the high cost of living on the island. "It wasn't a raise at all, it turned out. It was more of a lateral move financially."

## HOUSING:

Upon Tony's arrival to Oahu, he secured a temporary room rental from a Hawaiian woman. When the rest of the family arrived, Tony vacated his rented room and rented a vacation house in Ewa Beach for his family. While looking for more permanent housing, Tony and Kelly focused on neighborhoods that were "very haole" in their makeup and eventually found housing near the military base. During the course of their search for permanent housing, they learned that non-Hawaiians should not and do not move to the area of Waianae, on the west side of the island, because of the hostility toward them. However, Kelly discovered throughout her time on Oahu that the Hawaiian native population was generally accepting of haoles.

> Tony and Kelly focused on neighborhoods that were "very haole" in their makeup and eventually found housing near the military base.

After spending more time on the island, Kelly found the North Shore to be more desirable for her family because it was less crowded and had lower housing costs than other parts of the island. The commute to the Honolulu area, where Tony's job was, from the North Shore would have been nearly an hour, so it was never an option for them to live in that area of the island.

After three and a half years on Oahu, Kelly and Tony purchased a home in Ewa Beach because they believed they would live on the island for a long time. However, the day after closing on their new home, Tony was laid off and thus began the plans to move back to the mainland. Kelly shared, "I wanted him to find employment on Oahu, but Tony was frustrated by his layoff; he wanted to move back to the mainland, so we packed up and returned."

Unfortunately, Kelly and Tony never did move into their new Oahu home. After a short burst of unsuccessful efforts to sell their house in Oahu, they decided to rent it out instead of selling.

## SCHOOLING:

Kelly and Tony didn't have to concern themselves with schools. Kelly homeschooled her oldest daughter; and when her son reached school age, she homeschooled him, too. The youngest child was born in

Hawaii, via midwives at home, and the family moved off the island prior to her reaching school age. Kelly and Tony never did utilize day care for their children.

Though Kelly homeschooled her children and didn't have any firsthand experience about the schools in Hawaii, she said, "It was well known not to place your children in school in Waianae. Haoles are not accepted and you will get beat up if you are white." Kelly found

Kelly with her newborn baby

that the schools near the military base were safer for non-Hawaiians because there were more mainland military children in the schools.

## ACTIVITIES:

Kelly and Tony took advantage of Hawaii's natural topography by going to the beach, whale watching, and hiking. They often barbecued

The family visiting Volcanoes National Park on the Big Island

and swam at White Plains Beach and Pu'uloa Beach, both of which were within walking distance of their Ewa Beach home and where there were often birthday parties and other family gatherings. The Ko'Olina Resort near Ewa Beach has a lagoon that they frequented because there were no waves or lava rocks.

The family also took in tourist attractions like the Honolulu Zoo, Pearl Harbor, the *USS Missouri*, and Bishop Museum.

## SOCIALIZATION AND INTEGRATION:

Though Kelly and Tony moved to a more haole-populated part of the island, Kelly still felt hostility from the Hawaiian population and remembers one time being aggressively confronted for no reason. But that wasn't the case with all of the Hawaiians. "I had Hawaiian friends. I did have local friends, too, who were not of Hawaiian descent but were born on the islands. I also had haole friends that included Puerto Ricans, Caucasians, Blacks, Asians, and Filipinos."

Through Kelly and Tony's church, Hope Chapel Kapolei, they were welcomed and befriended. Kelly shared, "That is where I made most of my friends. I did use them to familiarize myself to the island. I learned many things in regards to where to go and hang out, where not to go . . . cultural things as well." Their children also attended Awana (http://www.awana.org/), a Bible group where children learn about Jesus through fun activities.

Kelly also started attending a homeschool group, Ewa Beach Homeschoolers; however by the time she joined, she was almost due to have a baby so she did not get very involved.

## HELPFUL RESOURCES:

"The biggest resource was learning from others who lived there," Kelly shared. She and Tony found their realtor by chance when calling a real estate office about a rental property they were interested in. This realtor later helped them purchase a property, and eventually they became friends.

Tamura's Market in Hau'ula was also a great find for Kelly. "After seeing how low Tamura's Market prices were, I continued to shop there and we saved quite a bit in groceries weekly."

## LIKES:

Kelly reminisced, "I like the weather. The rainbows . . . I love them and miss seeing them after the rains. The beaches . . . beautiful water . . . the massive volcanic rock mountains."

## DISLIKES:

The cost of air conditioning prevented Kelly and Tony from utilizing it as much as they wanted to. "It was okay when there were trade winds. Not so good when there were no trade winds. It took me about six months to get used to not having it. After that, I just rolled with it," Kelly confessed.

She also wished she could get in the car to go see her family, but instead she had to get on a plane and fly six or seven hours to see them. "It's an inconvenience to travel."

Kelly shared her intense frustration with Oahu's traffic. "Horrible traffic and no parking!!!!"

Aerial view of the Oahu Freeway Interchange

## BEST MOMENT:

When Kelly befriended a local hapa girl (mixed race/half Hawaiian), she began to feel like she belonged in Hawaii. "Teri embraced me as her friend! She loved me like a sister and would call me and allowed me to be a part of her life."

## REGRETS:

Although Kelly said that her move went well, if she were to do it over again, she would make more of an effort to move the whole family together. It would have been easier to all go at the same time . . . if we'd sold the house faster."

Kelly also wished they had not bought a house on Oahu; she realized, though, that if Tony had not lost his job, then the housing would have worked out well.

## ADAPTATION:

When Kelly lived in Ecuador as a child, she learned what it was like ". . . to live as an outsider and adapt to another culture." She later understood that Hawaii was like Ecuador in many ways. "I lived [in Hawaii] with the mental reality of living as a stranger in a foreign country." Knowing they would never be accepted like Hawaiians are, Kelly and her family adapted as much as haoles could.

Kelly and Tony knew their children had acclimated pretty well to island life. They loved going to the beach and playing outside, but Kelly and Tony weren't prepared for their children's reaction upon leaving Oahu. "The kids were crying in the car just before we left. They never cried like that before," Kelly said.

## BEST ADVICE:

If considering a move to Hawaii, Kelly insisted, "As long as you don't go there expecting things to be done your way and you respect their culture and their way of doing things, they will be more accepting of you." She also had a few other suggestions, listed below.

- ◆ Be open.

- ◆ Respect the people.

- ◆ Complain at home with your doors closed; then when you head outside, do it with a smile on your face.

## VERDICT:

Kelly would love to move back to Hawaii, but if given a choice, she would choose the Big Island because it is less crowded than Oahu. However, in order to do this, she and Tony would have to make some decisions about what to do eventually with the house they still own on Oahu. "God has a plan, and if it involves Hawaii, great, and if it doesn't, then that's okay, too."

Jordan and Whitney's favorite
beach was Black Sand Beach at
Wai'anapanapa State Park in Hana.
"[It has a] pretty sweet cave . . .
pretty sketchy and dark," he recalled.

Jordan and Whitney at Black Sand Beach

# CASE #47632: LIFE OUTSIDE THE BOX

**Perpetrator(s):** Jordan (22), Whitney (21)
**Accomplice(s):** None
**Time In Hawaii:** 4 Months
**Island:** Maui

## BACKGROUND:

Feeling restless at only 14 years old, Jordan left the confines of school to pursue a life *outside the box*. Shortly thereafter, he traveled with his sister to Maui and babysat for his nephew while she attended a retreat. That trip to Hawaii was the experience that forged his path outside the traditional American ideals. Although Jordan was young, he still remembers the experience. "I thought it was so beautiful," he said.

Several years later and after meeting Whitney in Sedona where they both resided, they talked frequently about embarking on an adventure, but then life took an unexpected turn. "We got into a terrible car accident. She was ejected and rolled over by the car. I was banged up with cuts . . . glass in my head—and was told she may not make it." After more than a month in the hospital, several months in a wheelchair, and intensive rehabilitation, Whitney learned to walk and read again.

After being in a bed and a wheelchair for so long, Whitney's longing for an adventure grew stronger than ever! Jordan reflected, "She's adventurous. She was saying, 'Let's go, let's go, let's go!'"

> "She's adventurous. She was saying, 'Let's go, let's go, let's go!'"

While at a fundraising event to cover costs for Whitney's medical expenses, Jordan came across a couple who told him about Worldwide Opportunities on Organic Farms, a company that helps to place volunteer workers (aka WWOOFers) on organic farms throughout the world. Jordan thought the opportunity would be the perfect answer to his and Whitney's desire to live life a little differently.

After applying for and being accepted to work on a Maui farm, Jordan purchased one-way tickets to Hawaii for both him and Whitney, and about one month later they departed for Maui for their four-month excursion.

## FINANCES:

Jordan and Whitney didn't set a specific financial goal prior to leaving for Maui, but they knew they had to have a little extra cash on hand. Though housing and some food were provided on the farm, they both still had to have money for any extra activities, food, and his monthly cell phone bill. In addition to that small fund, he and Whitney subsisted on the small stipend of $25 per week that they each received from the farm owner.

When Jordan originally purchased his one-way ticket, he was careful to reserve funds prior to leaving for the airline flight back.

Since the plan was to stay just a couple months, he and Whitney knew they'd be traveling back to Sedona.

## TRAVEL AND SHIPPING:

Because Jordan and Whitney didn't have a vehicle in Sedona, they didn't have to worry about shipping one to Maui. "We just took two really sweet backpacks with clothes, a knife, water bottles, and a laptop." Whitney managed to fill an extra bag with their yoga mats; they couldn't do without these on the island!

Since Whitney and Jordan didn't have a vehicle, he had to find a ride to the farm. "The farm owner picked us up at the airport . . . made a Costco run, then to a natural food store, then to Hana, about three hours away." Sitting in the back of the pick-up truck on the winding road to Hana was a bittersweet ride. "Whitney was super stoked . . . it was beautiful, moist . . . always such a treat coming from Arizona." The twists and turns took a toll on Jordan, leaving him vomiting over the side of the truck!

> "Whitney was super stoked . . . it was beautiful, moist . . . always such a treat coming from Arizona."

Jordan and Whitney remained on the farm for four months. The only time they left was when they rode with friends to Kahului. They then hopped on public transportation along with a little hitch-hiking to travel the island for a couple days, staying at a hostel and a hotel. Jordan reflected on not having a vehicle. "I had no desire to leave [the farm]." Therefore not having a vehicle did not pose a problem for them.

The owner of the farm went to Kahului weekly and would pick up items that the WWOOFers requested. Since the farm owners provided fruits, vegetables, rice, oats, and flour, the only food item that Jordan and Whitney had on their wish list was tortillas.

## EMPLOYMENT:

Being farm hands was the only employment Jordan and Whitney planned for their short stay on Maui. After getting a tip about organic farming, Jordan and Whitney were quick to place their application on the WWOOF website (http://www.wwoofusa.org/). They were soon contacted by the owners of Hana Tropicals, a 420-acre farm, who Jordan called *super nice*. "I had experience in landscaping. [We were] both into the organic movement—local food." Jordan also claimed that a good attitude is important when seeking this type of work. "[The farm owners] have so many applicants every day because it's an exclusive farm."

In addition to housing, electricity, water, and most of their food, Jordan and Whitney each received $25 per week after committing to a three-month stay on the farm. Jordan fell into the position of vegetable garden manager, which gained him unlimited access to vegetables. "There were a few super-big beds that we ate from . . . tons of bell peppers, eggplant, herbs, mangoes, guava . . . all the fruit that grows on the farm like bananas . . . tons of papayas the size of your head. We ate healthier than we usually did. I was healthier than I ever was in my life."

Jordan and Whitney stayed on the farm for four months, but Jordan claimed, "Some bailed out before then. If you are doing great on the farm, then you can stay as long as you want. The owners ask for courtesy with a notice to leave."

## HOUSING:

Housing was provided on the farm, but Jordan admitted the volunteer workers were *totally roughing it*. The property contained a double-wide container that Jordan compared to a freight train container, but with a foundation and drywall inside and a communal kitchen and two bedrooms. Also on the property was a renovated school bus with two bedrooms. The bathroom was a 30-foot walk to a warehouse that Jordan was happy to report *was not off-grid* so the toilets were fully functional!

Jordan harvesting papaya on the farm

After Jordan and Whitney investigated the many farms on Maui from afar, they settled in the Hana area because of its beauty. "[It's a] very scarcely populated jungle. So desolate, yet so full of life," he mused.

## SCHOOLING:

N/A

## ACTIVITIES:

Even without a vehicle, Jordan and Whitney were able to partake in what the island had to offer. "What an adventure it was. On our off-time we would walk to the beach and lie in the sun. We even managed to travel all over the island." They were also able to walk to the *tiny town of Hana* frequently and Hana Bay where they just *chilled,* but Jordan admitted that although it was the closest beach to the farm, it was their least favorite.

Jordan and Whitney's favorite beach was Black Sand Beach at Wai'anapanapa State Park in Hana. "[It has a] pretty sweet cave . . . it's pretty sketchy and dark," Jordan recalled. He also remembers

Jordan said he and Whitney often visited ". . . an awesome snorkeling spot behind Hana Bay."

walking in fresh water in the cave, crawling up rocks, and swimming through other parts. "It was pitch black." The swimming was better at Hamoa Beach according to Jordan, where he also surfed a few times.

"Red Sand Beach was a really sweet-ass beach . . . crystal clear water. It's a little hike in—so secluded. It's in a crescent shaped nook. Nudists are there all the time!" Jordan said.

## SOCIALIZATION AND INTEGRATION:

Jordan said that all of the socialization *came to us*. There was a farm a mile away that had fresh pizzas and beer every Friday and Saturday night. At those get-togethers, he and Whitney were able to meet many local residents. "They are super nice sweet people and are especially kind to WWOOFers . . . they know why you're there . . . they are not a fan of tourists."

On one occasion, a neighboring farm owner visited Hana Tropicals, where Whitney and Jordan worked, with two of the farm's volunteer workers. Oddly, Whitney knew them! The other WWOOFers were from Whitney's high school in Sedona!

## HELPFUL RESOURCES:

Since Jordan is a self-proclaimed minimalist, his goal is to need nothing at all times. "I'm not into stuff." This makes living on a secluded part of a remote island much easier than it would be for many other people. "There's no clothing [for sale in Hana] . . . have to go to Kahului. Never needed anything . . . although my flip flops got pretty bad." He hitched a ride to Pai'a to purchase a new pair.

## LIKES:

Jordan liked the weather, beauty, and produce that Maui offered. "It's the most incredible produce I ever had. You plant a seed and within 24 hours it sprouts! Everything flourishes there—even without watering! You can literally watch some specials grow!"

Jordan at the farm getting ready to hang the nearly 100 pounds of harvested bananas he chopped down

## DISLIKES:

Living on a farm placed Jordan and Whitney among the worst conditions for bugs. "The centipedes are everywhere . . . all over flowers . . . tons in the vegetable garden . . . hiking." But Jordan is relieved that he has never been bitten.

"There are big-ass rats the size of children . . . and they're ugly!" Jordan remembered. "The mosquitoes are so big you can feel them biting you! They are not on my good list. Mosquitoes suck . . . and I am not into centipedes!"

In addition to the insects, Jordan felt it was inconvenient to leave the island for any reason. "It's a hassle to go anywhere."

## BEST MOMENT:

When Jordan arrived on Maui, he remembered saying, "This is awesome!" As previously mentioned, while on his way to Hana in the back of a pick-up truck taking in the beautiful view, he got sick. "I was puking over the edge of the truck. After one of the final bridges, I told the driver to pull over." Even though he was throwing up on the side of the road to Hana, Jordan was still in awe of his surroundings.

## REGRETS:

Jordan wished he had better knowledge of what to expect upon his arrival to the island. "I would not know unless I experienced it. It's impossible to know." However, sharing his experience will help others relocate with more information.

## ADAPTATION:

Jordan reflected on his short stay on Maui. "I feel like moving anywhere . . . the first couple nights you're in shock. I adapted super well. I experienced the Hawaiian culture when I interacted with the locals. I adapted to a small town by going to get-togethers."

Jordan said there were a few things that were difficult to adapt to. "It's hard to get used to the humidity and mosquitoes. I walked into a swarm of mosquitoes and was bit 100+ times. I took supplements to help [like] B12 and peppermint oil."

## BEST ADVICE:

Jordan thinks positively when offering his advice, listed below, to others who want to move to Hawaii.

- Just do it!

- Be super-grateful.

- ◆ Have a great time.

- ◆ You should really think seriously about moving to avoid wasting as little time as possible.

## VERDICT:

Sedona pulled Whitney and Jordan back, but he claimed it wasn't because of island fever or the hundreds of daily mosquito bites. "It was something else . . . something that managed to pull us right back to Sedona."

Going back to Maui is on Jordan's to-do list. "I will absolutely go back. I am working so much now [as a cook in Sedona] and learning so much. Life is incredible now. I'm excited to find passion. I want to exhaust that while I have the urge to cook." He

Jordan at the farm opening coconuts to drink the fluid

would even consider WWOOFing again, unless he just visits the island for a few weeks of vacation. "I would visit everyone in Hana!"

The roosters on the island are not one of Gina's favorite things. "They are absolute nuisances. They crow all hours of the day or night."

Gina horseback riding at CJM Stables in Poipu

# CASE #42118: COME HELL OR HIGH WATER

**Perpetrator(s):** Gina (50), Mark* (56)
**Accomplice(s):** None
**Time In Hawaii:** 10.5 Years
**Island:** Kauai

## BACKGROUND:

Gina was a frequent traveler to Hawaii and had visited several times without her husband Mark. He hated flying so he refused to get on a plane, but Gina's love for the islands kept her persistent. She was finally able to convince him to go with her, and after that first trip, they went back to Kauai together every year. Each year they talked about relocating to Hawaii from the San Francisco, California area. "We were like little kids at summer camp . . . we were in tears when we left [Hawaii]."

When Gina's in-laws died suddenly, she claimed, "It was a bit of a wake-up call." If she and Mark were going to make the move, they thought it needed to be sooner than later. On Gina's 40th birthday,

---

* *Name Has Been Changed.*

they decided to relocate to Kauai. With no financial plan in place, they put their house on the market and set a target date to move. "Come hell or high water, we're moving to Kauai," Gina remembered saying. She gave notice to her employer, a phone company, while Mark arranged with his employer to continue working at his job in technology from a distance. "People thought we were crazy saying, *Who leaves good jobs to go to an island?*"

Gina and Mark followed their hearts instead of the advice of others. They purchased round-trip tickets, and a few short months later, they arrived on Kauai just one day after they'd signed papers to initiate the sale of their home.

## FINANCES:

The hope that Gina and Mark's house had doubled in price since they had purchased it six years earlier came true. They were able to make enough money from the sale of their house to fund their entire relocation, including a down payment on a house on Kauai but not without some pressure during the home selling process. "We got an offer the day we flew out [to Kauai] and signed papers to close [the transaction] on Kauai at Poipu Title Company." Gina said the house didn't sell as quickly as she and Mark had hoped it would, but they were relieved it didn't take much longer than it did (six months from initial offer to final closing). "Our house was our savings," Gina shared thankfully.

## TRAVEL AND SHIPPING:

Gina had heard horror stories about shipping belongings to Hawaii. "We had a humongous garage sale and gave away a lot of things to friends and just came with clothes."

She and Mark shipped one vehicle two weeks prior to their departure date through Matson (http://www.matson.com/) for $1000.

"We were having dinner at Dukes in Lihue at the harbor, and I see my car coming on a barge." She insisted it was her vehicle, but her husband said there was no way that it was her vehicle. "I raced back to the vacation rental, got binoculars, and went and looked at the license plate and, sure enough, it was my vehicle. I had that car for 20 years. It was like seeing an old friend."

In addition to shipping their vehicle, Gina and Mark took several suitcases on the plane with them. "We got killed [financially] for extra luggage. We had four or five bags each."

## EMPLOYMENT:

When Gina and Mark decided to put their home on the market on the mainland, they seriously considered relocating to the Big Island instead of Kauai because of the higher availability of jobs, but Kauai drew them in. "Something was pulling us to the island; I had a sense of belonging I never experienced before," Gina remembered. The draw was so strong that Gina was willing to give up the full retirement benefits that she would have earned if she had stayed at her job in California for only three more years!

> "I wanted to kick back a little while . . . but I got bored. It was fun to sleep in, take long walks . . . but it got old."

After Gina quit her job of 22 years on the mainland, she didn't feel pressured to quickly find a job when she moved to Kauai. "I wanted to kick back a little while . . . but I got bored. It was fun to sleep in, take long walks . . . but it got old."

Looking for jobs via *The Garden Island Newspaper*, Gina found a part-time position as an assistant to the director for that same newspaper about three months after her arrival on Kauai. However, ultimately the goal was to get a full-time job. "I liked the social outlet; I met lots of friends. I needed that."

Gina tried to gain employment with the state and Kauai County by taking tests for clerical positions but said she found out quickly that neither the state nor the county hired a lot of outsiders (newcomers). Gina did end up securing a part-time clerical job in the police department, but she still tried to find a full-time position. Soon thereafter, the state did contact her and offered her a full-time clerical position with the family courts, which she accepted. That is where she stayed for a couple years. About this time, Gina and Mark decided to relocate to the Big Island. She was luckily able to transfer with the state but didn't get the same position she had on Kauai. "It was a full-time temporary position in traffic court. I enjoyed it; I processed tickets."

After Gina spent a few months working in traffic court, she got a permanent full-time job with the drug court. Gina kept this job for about a year up until she and Mark moved back to Kauai.

Upon returning to Kauai, Gina secured a position at a preschool that she found advertised on Craigslist. At this writing, Gina has been employed at the preschool for about five years.

> "I worked in corporate America [on the mainland]. In ten years, I had half-a-dozen jobs [in Hawaii]. That's out of the norm for me."

Gina reflected on her employment history in Hawaii. "I worked in corporate America [on the mainland]. In ten years, I had half-a-dozen jobs [in Hawaii]. That's out of the norm for me."

Mark, on the other hand, arranged in advance with his employer to telecommute (with no relocation expenses paid), which was not a common way to work at the time of his and Gina's relocation. "He was the first employee in the division allowed to work from home." According to Gina, the move was a lateral one financially, and because of the high cost of living in northern California, the move was easy financially. "It wasn't as drastic as a Midwest relocation," Gina computed. Mark is still working with the same company, which Gina calls their *savior*.

## HOUSING:

Prior to leaving the mainland, Gina and Mark reserved vacation rentals for their first few weeks on the island. The first rental in Lihue Gina described as *a very nice lady's guest cottage.* Gina recalled her feelings from that first night so long ago. "We felt like little kids. We couldn't get to sleep. We were so excited to be here." She also remembered the woman who rented the vacation rental to them. "She made us chocolate chip cookies; she was really nice." Gina and Mark stayed there for three nights.

> "We felt like little kids. We couldn't get to sleep. We were so excited to be here."

Gina and Mark's next vacation rental was in Wailua Homesteads, where they stayed for five nights. Gina remembers this property vividly. "[This is] where I encountered my first cockroach. UGH!"

A condo rental in Princeville was the next vacation property that Gina and Mark stayed at, and this time it was for a few weeks. It was while they were in this vacation rental that they scoured the island for available long-term housing options. Although they were prepared financially to purchase a property, they decided to rent instead until they understood the island and its neighborhoods a little better.

Gina and Mark were aiming to live in Kapaa permanently, and when they frequented the town and walked around on foot, they asked random people if they knew of any long-term rentals in the area. That is how they got a referral for a long-term rental property, but it wasn't going to be available for two to three months. Therefore, they had to move to yet another vacation rental in Kapaa until the long-term rental property became available. When the property was finally ready, Gina and Mark signed a one-year lease for the two-bedroom and two-bathroom house in Wailua Houselots on Kauai's eastside for $2500 per month.

In Gina's opinion, house prices were still reasonable at the time she and Mark relocated to Kauai. She admitted to being bored without a job, so she kept busy by going to open houses. It was at an open house that she befriended a real estate agent. The agent began taking Gina around the island a few times a week to look at houses. Gina ended up finding a house she wanted to buy just a month after she and Mark moved into their long-term rental in Wailua Houselots! The landlord of their new rental was gracious enough to allow a sublease where the rental house could be re-rented to someone else. Two months later, they moved into their new home in Wailua Homesteads, also on the Eastside of the island.

> "I loved the Big Island. It's a good community . . . neighborly."

About three years later, Gina and Mark decided to sell their home on Kauai in order to move to the Big Island because of the *amazing home prices*. Also, Mark could have his piano shipped from the mainland if they had a bigger house. They sold their home on Kauai and made a substantial profit. They put those funds back into a home purchase about 10 minutes from downtown Hilo in the Kaiwiki neighborhood on the Big Island. Gina reminisced, "I loved the Big Island. It's a good community . . . neighborly." Unfortunately, though, the piano didn't make it. "The movers dropped the piano, and it was damaged and had to be shipped back to New York in order to repair it."

Almost three years and several trips to Kauai later, Gina and Mark found themselves missing that island tremendously. They decided to move back to Kauai, along with their repaired piano. Gina confessed, "The Big Island doesn't have the beaches that Kauai has." They sold their house in Hilo and took a loss. Plus Gina and Mark had a new addition to their family when they moved back to Kauai—an 11-pound Chihuahua-Terrier mix. "She is eight years old and is very clean and mellow."

> Gina confessed, "The Big Island doesn't have the beaches that Kauai has."

In the market for a rental once again on Kauai, Gina and Mark were able to find a long-term rental house. It was a two-bedroom house with a pool in Wailua Homesteads for $2500 per month, and they signed a six-month lease. Unfortunately, the sale on the Hilo home was not quick enough, and they had to endure maintaining two house payments, one on each island, for a couple months.

In their new Kauai rental property, the monthly cost of electricity was $300. This surpassed the monthly norm of $150 per month because of the high cost of operating and maintaining a pool. Gina and Mark quickly grew tired of the high electric bill, so they started looking for a property that would cost less per month. They found a newly built two-bedroom and two-bathroom townhouse in Lihue near Costco. They signed a month-to-month lease for $1800 per month and stayed in that townhouse for about three months. They decided to leave because they weren't happy living in such close proximity to neighbors.

Once again, Gina went house shopping and found a 1970s fixer-upper house in Wailua Homesteads. After purchasing the house, she and Mark ". . . gutted the whole thing. It was a nice house and a nice neighborhood." Gina said she *loved it!* But that didn't stop them from moving again! "Since my hubby works from home, he did not like all the noise he heard during the day since we lived in a regular neighborhood that was close to the main road." They stayed in the house for about four years and broke even financially when they sold it.

Gina and Mark found another house to buy on five acres with a guest cottage in Wailua Homesteads. Because of the large number of improvements being done on the property, they are temporarily renting a vacation house in Moloa'a near Larson's Beach until it is completed. "Although we wanted to stay in Kapaa, the rental market [inventory] right now is quite low, not to mention 90 percent of [the landlords] refuse to take pets, even with an extra pet deposit." Luckily, the landlord agreed to Gina and Mark's mild-mannered dog. For a mere $3000 per month, Gina and Mark are staying in that temporary Moloa'a two-bedroom and two-bathroom cottage.

## SCHOOLING:

To integrate into the Hawaiian culture and also because of pure fascination, Mark enrolled at Kauai Community College when he and Gina first arrived so he could learn the Hawaiian language. Gina said he has almost lost the language now because it has been so long since he took the class; however when he sees a Hawaiian word, he does a good job of pronouncing it.

Gina took several classes that the preschool offered through a service called PATCH (http://patchhawaii.org/), an organization that offers child care training classes.

## ACTIVITIES:

Gina and Mark participate in the neighborhood community meetings (*not* a homeowners' association group). That's where the neighbors talk and make plans for the parks and the roads in the immediate area. "It gives us a common interest." Mark has even testified at council meetings when he felt strongly about issues, which Gina said is *out of the norm* for him. The local television stations even televise the meetings.

Mark joined a paddle team at the Pu'uwai Canoe Club for a brief time. When he belonged to the group, they would often go up and down the Wailua River. One day the group took the canoes out to the ocean and his tipped over. Gina proclaimed, "This did spook him due to the shark issue. He freaked out, so he doesn't do it now!"

Gina and Mark both enjoy hiking and going to the beach. One of her favorite hikes is the Sleeping Giant Trail, also known as the Nounou Trail. "It's a good workout; at the top are awesome views." One of the houses they rented in Wailua Houselots was right next to the trail! Their favorite beach is near the Beach House Restaurant in Poipu in South Kauai. "The snorkeling is awesome!" Gina claimed, and said that it's the best snorkeling on the island.

Gina admitted she and Mark don't take advantage of what Kauai has to offer. "We know it's here, but it's always going to be here. We get spoiled," Gina realized.

## SOCIALIZATION AND INTEGRATION:

Gina and Mark *are not drinkers* so they don't like to attend many social events. "We meet people passing by; we get invited places." Gina admitted to being more social than Mark. "I miss my close-knit set of friends. I could count on one hand who is my friend here."

One of Gina's friends on Kauai told her, "Lots of local folks know transplants will leave, so they won't invest time and energy in you." Gina said that some people assume she's local because of the way she looks so they start talking to her. "Hawaiians will talk Pidgin to me, and when I speak, they realize I'm not from here. Hawaiians are very guarded," Gina advised. "Rightfully so—they're very protective of [the island]."

## HELPFUL RESOURCES:

Gina claimed word of mouth is the best resource on the island. Her friends who work with her at the preschool give her referrals when needed. She also questions others to give her the scoop on other things.

Gina continues to use Craigslist frequently. It served her well when she was looking for housing. She has also bought and sold household items via Craigslist. When she has something that she no longer wants, she usually lists it for free, and the item gets picked up very quickly. Gina said that newcomers ask if it is safe to use Craigslist. Gina confessed to often being home alone when strangers arrive to purchase something she listed on Craigslist. "Everyone is so guarded on the mainland about Craigslist. Because it's an island . . . crime is less."

## LIKES:

The serenity of Kauai is what first comes to mind when Gina thinks about the island. "I like the peace, beauty, beaches . . . the calmness that it gives me." Reflecting on her life on the mainland, Gina said, "I used to be one of the rat race people. I have to stop [now] and *talk story*—take a deep breath. It reminds you . . . where are you going and why are you in a hurry?" ("Talk story" is a Hawaiian phrase that means "an informal chat.")

Gina remembered when she first moved to Kauai. "I got in the longest line at the grocery store to learn patience. I love the transformation Kauai has given me."

## DISLIKES:

Gina misses not having the large group of friends she had while living on the mainland. "I miss going to San Francisco Giants' games with [them]." Gina does cherish the few new friends she has made in the last 10 years of living on Kauai.

Gina expressed another feature of Kauai she dislikes: "Obviously . . . bugs, centipedes, cockroaches! You can keep them at bay if you can use pesticides . . . pay for a quarterly service." Since Gina started using Mokihana Pest Control, Inc., she hasn't seen the bugs in the house. "It's like a steel wall they can't cross." She admitted that she once saw a humungous cockroach on the wall but said it was close to the time pest spraying was due. One even flew into her hair! Gina's suggestion: "Invest in a 50-cent fly swatter at Ace Hardware." Gina's centipede experience wasn't much bet-

A cane spider visiting Gina in her kitchen

ter. "A huge centipede was crawling toward me; I couldn't move . . . I was petrified—like in a horror movie. I screamed and screamed, yelling for my husband!" Mark was able to capture the centipede in a jar, take it outside, and cut off its head.

The roosters on the island are other adversaries of Gina's. "They are absolute nuisances. They crow all hours of the day or night. It's like nonstop barking dogs—the exact same thing. But it's high pitched and annoying." Gina does admit a bright side to roosters. "They eat centipedes, so they're nice to have."

Gina, a movie buff, is disappointed that newly released movies only run for one week. "You practically have to drop everything in order to see them." She often has to wait until the movies are released on DVD to watch them.

## BEST MOMENT:

When Gina and Mark spent their first night in Lihue eating chocolate chip cookies specially made for them, she knew then and there that they had made the right decision. "It was a neat feeling."

One of Gina and Mark's long-term landlords, a German lady, invited them for brunch and a hike after they signed the lease. "There's something about Kauai—you could take a not-so-nice person and, guaranteed . . . [he or she] will make a transformation."

Wrapping up her thoughts on Kauai, Gina shared, "[Today] is my 51st birthday, and as I was driving to work this morning, I was blessed with a double rainbow crossing the Wailua Bridge in Kapaa. Wow! What an awesome sight first thing in the morning. The main rainbow was so bright and vibrant, I thought a space ship was going to suck me up from the sky! I wish I would [have] had time and room to pull over to take a picture but, as our local weather guy always says, *It's just another day in paradise!*"

## REGRETS:

After over 10 years on Kauai, Gina reflected on her time on the island and quickly concluded there weren't any regrets. Her leaving initially was difficult for her parents, but she was finally able to convince her parents to visit just last year and they *loved it.*

## ADAPTATION:

Coming from a culture in San Francisco that's *every man for himself,* Gina believes that she and Mark adapted to the slower pace. "When it comes to Kauai, you slow down, you stop and smell the plumerias. It makes you pause—to appreciate the environment."

Although Gina and Mark have adjusted to the island lifestyle, she admitted that the hardest part has been not having friends. "My husband can go without friends," Gina said, but added that she couldn't.

## BEST ADVICE:

Since Gina and Mark relocated three times in Hawaii, including once to Kauai, then to the Big Island, then back to Kauai, their experiences have led Gina to offer some sound advice, listed below.

- Definitely do not move if you have any debt.

- Get rid of your possessions.

- Keep an open mind.

- Hawaii is not for everybody.

- Have patience.

- Save money to cover at least six months of expenses in case you can't find a job right away.

- Leave your pets behind.

## VERDICT:

Gina insisted, "I will definitely die here. I love it here that much . . . even when I'm shopping [for a house] and realize we could live in a mansion in any other state [for $500,000]."

Mark recently asked Gina if she wanted to move back to the mainland, and her response was, "HELL NO!" He is now on the same page as she is, especially since they found a *sweet* property.

Dawn enjoys the many farmers' markets and festivals with her family throughout the year

Dawn and Doug

# CASE #21612: FROM HILLBILLY TO HIPPIE

**Perpetrator(s):** Dawn (42), Doug (40)
**Accomplice(s):** Son (5) And 13 Show Dogs
**Time In Hawaii:** 3 Months
**Island:** Big Island

## BACKGROUND:

Since Dawn married Doug eight years ago in Gatlinburg, Tennessee, he never stopped reminding her that one day they would move to the Big Island. As a matter of fact, it was a prerequisite for their marriage, and this was suitable for Dawn since they were both *country people*. Eighteen years prior to the family relocating to Hawaii, Doug lived on the Big Island and on Maui for a total of 10 years. After falling in love with the Big Island back then, he purchased five acres of land in the Hilo area with plans to make it his home someday. That day arrived.

Besides discussing moving plans, Dawn and Doug didn't get serious about actual planning until four years prior to the move. The first thing on Dawn's mind was her job, a performance act with her

13 dogs, and whether or not she could transport them and continue performing in Hawaii. A few vacations weren't enough for Dawn to commit to moving, so on a crisp Tennessee day shortly after Christmas, she took a trip to the Big Island by herself to ". . . discover and feel it out and get a vibe for the area." Although Doug had been pushing Dawn for eight years to move, that trip motivated her more. "I came back and said that I don't care, let's just do it. I was more carefree than Doug at that point."

Dawn purchased a house on that trip by herself and soon she and Doug, their five-year-old son, and 13 dogs were on their way to the Big Island.

## FINANCES:

Although they did not plan methodically, Dawn and Doug did arrive in Hawaii with a *substantial* savings account. However, Dawn confesses to wishing she had paid more attention to the financial aspects of the move and saved more money. The end result was that she and Doug spent more than they thought they would.

> Dawn confesses to wishing she had paid more attention to the financial aspects of the move and saved more money.

Dawn currently puts that savings into play when she grocery shops. "If you hit the sales, it's the same price as back home. If it's not on sale, just don't buy it. You don't buy the things you used to buy. I go bargain shopping . . . two to three stores in one day."

Doug and Dawn were shocked upon their arrival in Hawaii to learn that the items they thought would be expensive were not, and items they didn't think would be expensive were. For example, Dawn thought that cleaning and baking supplies, and wine would be expensive, but they weren't. On the other hand, she didn't realize how expensive soups, canned vegetables, cheese, juice, dog food, and Lunchables would be.

## TRAVEL AND SHIPPING:

Over the course of six months, Dawn spoke to every airline company, sometimes more than once, to get the information she needed about transporting her 13 performance dogs, because, after all, that was the way she made a living. If she didn't get an answer she liked, she would call and speak to a different person. Dawn shared, "It's very frustrating getting current information, but Alaska was by far the friendliest and most accommodating airline."

Dawn's performing dogs dressed up for Christmas

An employee in the cargo department even called Dawn back with some alternative ideas for transporting the dogs. During all of her calls to Alaska Airlines, the employees remained friendly and helpful.

For the first step of travel, Dawn's mother assisted by flying Dawn's five-year-old son to Oakland, California. Dawn and her friend focused on driving the dogs from Tennessee to Oakland. Upon arrival in Oakland, they all stayed at a dog-friendly hotel near the airport (yes, with all of the animals). The next morning, Dawn's friend caught an early flight to Kona, Hawaii, with five of the dogs checked in the cargo area and one dog under the seat. With only one direct flight to Kona every other day, Dawn, her son, and the remaining dogs took the next flight out two days later with a dog under her seat, a dog under her son's seat, and five checked in as cargo. Dawn's mom then dropped Dawn's car off to Matson (http://www.matson.com/), a shipping company, to be shipped to Hawaii before she went back to Tennessee. Dawn insists that flying out of Oakland can be a good central point to meet if transporting cars because although Matson has a branch in Los Angeles, it's much more expensive to fly to Hawaii out of Los Angeles compared to Oakland. Cargo is very expensive so placing any animals under one's seat is a better option. Dawn paid $100 per dog for each one she placed under the seat.

> Cargo is very expensive so placing any animals under one's seat is a better option.

Besides transporting the dogs to Hawaii, there were questions about quarantine. Dawn did research on the Hawaii Department of Agriculture website (http://hdoa.hawaii.gov/) and found that if an animal owner begins exercising the Hawaiian quarantine requirements eight months before relocating the animal to Hawaii, that the animal can then meet the Hawaiian health requirements and skip the quarantine process, qualifying the animal for a direct release, which means the animal can go directly home with the owner once landing in Hawaii. Dawn said disbelievingly, "Most people are not knowledgeable about that aspect of transporting animals," which she found out when she ran her Facebook campaign, Homeward Bound Hounds, a documentary of transporting her dogs to Hawaii. "We received a lot of backlash for putting our dogs through the quarantine process. It made me much more aware how many people don't know that's not the case."

The expenses for transporting the dogs:

◆ Permits for direct release cost $145 per dog.

◆ The rabies titer tests were $85 per dog.

- ◆ Health certificates were $38 per dog.

- ◆ Check-in service for the dogs at Kona airport was $150 for the first dog and $50 for each additional dog. It is higher for nights and weekends.

Overall, the average price to transport one dog for direct release would be $550 to $600 if they didn't go cargo.

Dawn used Kona Veterinary Service to check in the dogs, one of two veterinarian clinics that can check in direct-release animals. "I LOVED the veterinarian, and she was such a help in getting me the information and support I needed!" Dawn exclaimed.

Dawn and Doug shipped everything they owned, including two vehicles. They even stocked up on and shipped *costly* items and shipped them to avoid purchasing them on the island.

The transporting of the shipping container was seamless using Matson, but there were a few issues with getting one of their vehicles from Tennessee to Matson in Oakland. Dawn and Doug couldn't use some of the available vehicle transportation companies for one of their vehicles because it was too tall. There was a wait list for spaces that could accommodate taller vehicles and, consequently, they had no definite delivery date. They ended up driving the vehicle themselves to Matson instead

Dawn's and Doug's son playing with the dogs

of dealing with the mainland vehicle transportation hassles. Again, weather can cause delays, and a hurricane in the Pacific Ocean delayed the car for a few days, which caused extra expense renting a car for a longer period.

Dawn stayed in Tennessee to complete the travel arrangements, and Doug made his way to the Big Island so he could get a jump-start on preparing their new home in Hawaii. He was able to move right into the house they had purchased several months earlier. The shipping crate from Matson arrived just a day later.

The few things they needed since their arrival have been expensive, like furniture and decorative household items. Craigslist is ". . . pretty pricey for used things, and there isn't a lot of variety," Dawn revealed.

## EMPLOYMENT:

Doug arranged ahead of time to continue his job as a geologist online and at a distance, although the distance part is only temporary. He will be faced with finding a new job eventually. Dawn is planning to continue performing with the dogs. She has already begun working at a kennel and has already had two performing jobs, including one at the county fair. When asked what they will do if Doug cannot find work, Dawn responded matter-of-factly, "We will NEVER move back to the mainland. It's not an option."

## HOUSING:

When Dawn visited the Big Island eight months prior to her move, she was not on vacation. She spent the majority of the time visiting schools, different areas of the island, and specific neighborhoods. She narrowed her options for housing by realizing she needed land for the dogs and that they probably would not find a landlord who would rent to a family with 13 dogs. So the house hunt began near the Hilo area, which is more rural than most parts of the island and it fit the *country feel* they desired.

The initial plan was to build on the five acres Doug purchased a long time ago, but because building can be such a slow process and

The family at their house in Pahoa

because it's tough to manage it from afar, Doug and Dawn waited until they made a permanent move to the island. They purchased a prebuilt house to live in until they have completed the building on their property.

During Dawn and Doug's house hunting, they learned that many of the larger acreage properties like those in Orchid Land and Mountain View have unpaved roads that are not maintained by the county. Therefore, no bank would loan to them on those properties. This thwarted their plans because they did not have the cash to purchase a home without a bank loan. Instead, they found a home in the Hawaiian Beach subdivision in Pahoa that was less than an acre and not nearly the size of land they intended on purchasing.

Many of the houses in the Pahoa area are off-grid. Living off-grid is not very difficult for Dawn based on her past experiences, but she warned to be aware that if an area is off-grid, it will change the way you live.

## SCHOOLING:

Dawn and Doug's son attends kindergarten at Keonepoko Elementary School in Pahoa. Dawn is pleased with the homework that comes home and is seeing *incredible* progress thus far. The school has RAP, Hawaii's Read Aloud Program, which assists parents in reading with their children to promote a love of reading.

Dawn was shocked to learn that Keonepoko was so large, with five kindergarten classes, but the class sizes remain generally small, at least for kindergarten. Her son has only 18 students in his class, and they are mostly local Hawaiians. Dawn feels that the teacher is *wonderful* and seems to be *doing a great job!*

## ACTIVITIES:

Life for Dawn and Doug is much simpler now. They have more time in nature and for gardening and just playing. Their son spends a lot more time outside and enjoys his new tree swing. The family even made a fort out of palm fronds.

The weather permits daily outdoor activities, such as walking in the neighborhood, gardening, visiting Volcano National Park, and the occasional stop at Black Sand Beach.

## SOCIALIZATION AND INTEGRATION:

Dawn and Doug moved without knowing anyone on the island; therefore their social lives have not gotten off to a great start. Dawn loves her neighborhood and said, "Everyone is super friendly." The neighbors talk to them often, and one even brought them oranges. "But my husband thinks most people are negative, at least more so than what he remembers from 20 years ago," Dawn shared. "It's tough to meet people. Neither one of us has a traditional job. We don't go to a church. We are not out in the community much."

Dawn hopes that she can meet other families through her son's school. "I'd like to meet some other parents," she said, but the parents have not yet initiated communication. "It's not like they're being offish; it's probably because I'm new, and they don't know me. They're probably all friends from preschool." Happily, Dawn hasn't experienced any type of dislike or aggression from Hawaiians toward her or other mainlanders.

In order to get to know other families, Dawn is starting to volunteer at the school for events like the recent Fall Festival. Brandon has many friends at school and hasn't suffered as much as Dawn in the area of socialization. "He has several Hawaiian friends and non-Hawaiian friends," she shared. "I haven't seen any bullying of any kind."

Making street art outside Pele's Kitchen in downtown Pahoa

## HELPFUL RESOURCES:

Prior to the move, Dawn counted on Doug's prior knowledge of the island to a certain extent and used various Internet sources to gain information about schools and neighborhoods. She used a website (http://www.alohaliving.com/) to find a real estate agent. After the move, Dawn found Amazon to be useful for items she needed that weren't available on the island.

## LIKES:

Dawn and Doug love the weather in Hawaii as well as the friendly and welcoming Aloha Spirit. They feel that the language and culture of Hawaii make them feel like they're in another country with a rich tradition, unlike any of the other states they lived in. They also enjoy the many farmers' markets and festivals with their family throughout the year.

## DISLIKES:

Although Dawn hasn't had any surprises with their move except for some minor price shocks, she admits to missing her friends and family. "I can't just drive and go see my friends." When Dawn and Doug's son wants to go see his grandmother, she finds it difficult to explain why they can't jump in the car and go.

Dawn has also had some relationship adjustments with her parents. "I don't have support from my family and friends. Most people think we are crazy to move somewhere where a gallon of milk costs $10. My relationship with my parents is practically ruined over this move." However, Doug's parents are supportive, which has helped with the transition.

## BEST MOMENT:

During the first week and a half of their relocation, Dawn drove the two hours to Kona for a dog performance. On the way back, she traveled on Saddle Road through the middle of the island. It was pitch black because there are no lights to interfere with the observatory on the volcano. "I felt as though I was driving in the stars . . . I had never seen a sky so filled with stars before." She was so moved, she pulled over and got out of her car in the chilly night air and sat on the hood of her car in amazement. "It was the first time I really thought about the fact I was in the middle of the ocean on an island . . . and there was nothing around us . . . it was just so brilliant. It's the most incredible place on earth . . . there were trillions of stars."

Dawn also finds wonder simply lying and listening to the rain and stopping to look at the ocean. "I have lived in Tennessee, New Jersey, and California, but I have found happiness in Hawaii."

## REGRETS:

Although Dawn did not have many housing options because of the land needed for the dogs, she wished she lived closer to the beach. "I never thought I'd care about the beach, but watching my son in the water . . . he loves the beach." They would go to the beach more often, but the dogs cannot be left alone that long.

Dawn and Doug experienced a smooth relocation to the Big Island. Their only wish is that they had saved more money and been more attentive to the costs associated with purchasing items on the island.

## ADAPTATION:

Three months into living in their new home, Dawn confessed she is ". . . still an eternal optimist." Jokingly, she said to check back in a year to see how she feels but added again, "It's not an option to move back for three reasons: it's bloody expensive; jobs we can't go back to; and I wouldn't be happy anywhere else. It's a different culture, like Costa Rica, and I like that. It's like a foreign country."

Dawn added, "Getting used to the mold, the fruit flies, it's hard. It's very excessive . . . trying to keep things clean. If we were in Kona, we probably wouldn't see [the mold] as much; it'd be brown," she said chuckling.

On the bright side, Dawn and Doug's son is adjusting well. "He's much more outgoing," Dawn said. "He's much more outdoorsy than we knew. He mentions it all the time that he loves Hawaii. He also loves the rain and the beach. He never had the same appreciation back home for the outdoors."

"I feel such a sense of awe for this state, and I'm so excited to live here," Dawn said.

## BEST ADVICE:

Dawn and Doug suggested the following preparations to facilitate a smooth move.

◆ Since the weather can alter plans, save a little money for the unexpected expenses. The car took a few more days and was delayed due to a storm, so that is one expense you need to be aware of; a rental car for a week can be expensive.

Dawn's first harvest of bananas on her and Doug's vacant land and future home site

◆ Hotels on the Hilo side of the island are sparse and expensive. Rental houses will be cheaper than hotels and will have more availability in the Hilo area. A bed and breakfast is also a good choice and usually less expensive and much nicer than the hotels.

◆ House hunt in person as opposed to from afar due to the variety and diversity in each neighborhood. Many of the homes on the Hilo side of the island are off-grid, which may not be made clear in an email communication.

◆ Do not rely on any transport company or others to provide all the correct information. Dawn expressed, "I was amazed at how many of them had the wrong information, which in turn would have cost me more money!"

## VERDICT:

Dawn admits that it would be tough to go back to the mainland after seeing her son bloom in Hawaii, and ". . . this is Doug's dream to be here."

Among Tory's favorite summer shore dives is at Three Tables in Pupukea and said she hasn't seen any sharks there yet!

Tory and Alex

# CASE #49757: FOLLOWING IN DAD'S FOOTSTEPS

**Perpetrator(s):** Tory (30), Alex (30)
**Accomplice(s):** None
**Time In Hawaii:** 8.5 Years
**Island:** Oahu

## BACKGROUND:

Vacationing in Hawaii while still in her mother's womb, Tory was destined to be attracted to the islands. Visiting again as a toddler perhaps unknowingly cemented her roots in Hawaii. A few visits to see her dad who had recently moved to Molokai further confirmed that Hawaii is where she wanted to live. "My dad retired to Molokai so I thought I'd spend summers there. He kept telling me to move and he'd help," Tory said. She decided to take him up on his offer.

Considering that jobs were very scarce on the island of Molokai, Tory knew she would have to choose another island for employment purposes. After visiting Maui and the Big Island, she set her sights on Oahu. "There are more [employment] opportunities on Oahu."

Tory's employer, a mortgage company in Tucson, Arizona, had a branch in Oahu. Unfortunately that branch had no available positions. Therefore Tory quit her job in Tucson and left for Molokai to spend a couple weeks with her dad. Soon they left for Oahu together to settle Tory in her new home.

## FINANCES:

Tory's dad had committed to helping her relocate to Oahu so she didn't have to save money for the move. "My dad helped a lot. He supported me for the first month. He paid for my apartment and plane ticket and stocked the refrigerator." Tory lived with limited furnishings for about six months until her dad had paid for and packed up all of her belongings in Tucson and shipped them to Oahu for her.

## TRAVEL AND SHIPPING:

In Tucson, Tory was living in a home owned by her dad. When she moved to Oahu, she left her belongings in the house. When her dad sold the home about six months later, he shipped Tory's vehicle and other belongings to her on Oahu. When the container of her belongings arrived, everything went into storage because her apartment did not have sufficient space for it. However, Tory was able to start using her vehicle right away and no longer had to walk or take the bus everywhere.

Since Tory had arrived on Oahu with only two suitcases, her dad took her shopping and bought some basics for her, including a futon, bed, and kitchen supplies. "Everything was from Walmart," Tory said.

## EMPLOYMENT:

Tory was without a job when she first arrived on Oahu, but shortly after her arrival, her former employer (the mortgage company) agreed to allow her to work remotely from home via a laptop computer until she found a job. She took advantage of being able to choose the hours she worked. "It was great. I worked primarily at night and went out and roamed the island during the day!"

After a couple of months working remotely, her employer unexpectedly had a position open at their Oahu branch, and Tory jumped at the chance to join the team. "It was low paying and not what I was looking for, but at least it was steady income and barely paid my bills. I was very lucky!" She kept the job for five years until the company closed when the mortgage crisis swept through the country. Luckily, another company stepped in within two weeks and hired all of the previous employees back, including Tory. She was only on unemployment for those two weeks out of the entire time she's been on Oahu.

Tory stayed with that new company for eight months before they also went under. However, this time she'd known in advance it was going to happen, so she started applying for jobs. She secured employment at a local bank and still works there as a loan

> "It's a great living, but it's hard to market and establish my business. I had a mentor who showed me the ropes."

officer, where she is responsible for originating residential mortgage loans. "It's a great living, but it's hard to market and establish my business. I had a mentor who showed me the ropes."

## HOUSING:

Tory and her dad flew to Oahu together after she visited Molokai for a couple of weeks. They stayed at a hotel in Waikiki for two nights, and then she moved into a temporary apartment for a month. "It was a cockroach infested studio by the zoo for $1800 per month. Waikiki is a different animal for renting . . . it's probably gone up since then."

Tory then found a more permanent one-bedroom apartment outside of Waikiki in Kapiolani for $1500 per month; it was the enclosed garage of someone's residence. She was there less than six months when a neighbor reported the homeowner (and landlord) for not having a permit to enclose their garage. "Illegal rentals are very common here," Tory said. She had to move abruptly.

> "Illegal rentals are very common here," Tory said.

Tory scrambled to find housing quickly and ended up securing a legal guest home in Alewa Heights near downtown Honolulu. Six months later she left for an odd reason. "[The landlord] asked me to change my deodorant because she could smell it, and she was very sensitive to smells. I had to use free and clear laundry detergent and household cleaners. It was too much for me, so I found another place at the Diamond Head Ambassador in Waikiki."

Tory was excited with her new housing situation. "It was right on the beach, ocean views, studio in a co-op. I was there for about one and a half years." She left because the rent was going to be increased to an amount that was too high for her.

Coincidentally, Tory found out that the owners of the illegal garage apartment she stayed at previously had availability in their legal apartment above the garage. She moved back in and stayed for about three years until she purchased a condominium.

Tory started looking for a condominium to purchase while in the garage apartment. "It was a difficult price range." Consequently, she had to look at neighborhoods that were farther away from the Honolulu area even though she knew her commute to work would be increased up to an hour each way. She finally purchased a two-bedroom condo in Ewa Beach.

After a few years in Ewa Beach, Tory met her husband and they eventually purchased a house in Kailua. When Tory initially arrived on Oahu, Kailua had been her first choice for a place to live. Also, it was only a 30-minute drive to Honolulu. "It's beautiful [in Kailua]. I fell in love with it when I first moved there. The house is smaller than the condo, but it's a 10-minute walk to the beach. It's a nice little town where you can ride your bike to the grocery store, dinner, or yoga. You don't have to leave [the area]."

Tory still owns the Ewa Beach condo and rents it out. She reflected on her housing history. "Kailua is now the seventh place I've lived over the past eight and a half years; hopefully, it's the last one!"

Tory admits to moving around a lot until she purchased her condo, but she doesn't want others to be discouraged and said

Tory and Alex's wedding

housing is actually fairly easy to find. "Everyone has an *auntie* renting out an ohana." ("Auntie" is an affectionate term used to show respect to elder females.)

## SCHOOLING:

Tory attended one semester at Kapiolani Community College near the Diamond Head area. The one thing she remembered was the oddity of needing a tuberculosis test to attend school.

Tory and Alex's garden where they grow tomatoes, arugula, peppers, onions, strawberries, and all sorts of herbs

## ACTIVITIES:

One of Tory's favorite activities is gardening. "It's a lot wetter on the *windward* (east) side of the island. I grow kale, arugula, and flowers; that's not possible in Ewa Beach." The drier climate makes gardening more difficult according to Tory.

Tory enjoys Makaha Beach on the *leeward* (west) side of the island where she can *chill out*. She also admits it's a good beach for paddle boarding and barbecues and says the west side has good beaches.

> Tory enjoys Makaha Beach on the *leeward* (west) side of the island where she can *chill out.*

Tory participated in many of the activities that Hawaii has to offer, including paddle boarding, diving, boat excursions, and hiking. Her most recent paddle boarding excursion was at Kailua Bay, and she warned, "Check conditions before you go. If there's wind, don't go."

Tory also did shore diving in Ewa Beach and said it's more enjoyable if there's no wind; she cautioned against the North Shore in the wintertime because the wind produces turbulent waters.

Tory and her husband scuba dive often and utilize Brian Mara, with Hawaii Reef Divers, to set up their dives from different boats. They usually leave from Waianae Boat Harbor but also dive out of Kewalo Basin Harbor in Honolulu. "In the summer there's excellent shore diving at Pupukea, Shark's Cove, and Three Tables," and added that she hasn't seen any sharks there yet! Tory suggested visiting Brian's Facebook page, Oahu Dive Mob, which posts times and dates of dives. "It's a fun group!"

Tory used to do a lot of hiking and enjoyed Mariner's Ridge on the east side of the island. "It's not super easy . . . but not advanced. It's shaded for a good majority of the hike, and it's not good in the rain. At the top of the ridge you can see the other side of the island."

## SOCIALIZATION AND INTEGRATION:

Tory met most others through her work but admitted she didn't feel welcomed being the only white girl among all her Hawaiian and Asian co-workers. "It was tough [because] it was a much older group. It was tough to make good, solid friends." However, Tory admitted that her co-workers finally did warm up to her right before the company closed. "I became their family."

When Tory found her present position at the bank she confessed, "I was an outsider coming into a clique. It was hard [for them] to let others in. It was hard getting accepted . . . like high school, but after a year, those girls were my best friends."

## HELPFUL RESOURCES:

Tory admitted she *jumped on a plane and left* and didn't do any research prior to her relocation. When she moved, the Internet was not what it is today so the only choice to advertise or find what she needed was through a newspaper.

"Everything you need is on Oahu," Tory admitted, but she had to use Amazon for some hard-to-find items. "We order everything from dish brushes to phone cases, shaving cream, wash cloths, headphones, the list goes on."

Tory also noticed that many stores have opened on Oahu that weren't there when she relocated. "Now there is Target, Walgreens, Victoria's Secret, Petco, T.J. Maxx, Whole Foods, and H&M." She shops for major items and bulk items at Costco and claimed, "It's so expensive anywhere else." She also suggested shopping for produce at farmers' markets because it's *fresh and cheap.*

Lately, Tory uses Craigslist for miscellaneous items like furniture and other household goods, and she said housing options are all over Craigslist.

## LIKES:

Though Tory doesn't surf, she likes to watch the *surf craze* at the North Shore. "Every winter the surf on the North Shore is HUGE; by huge I mean 25 feet plus! You don't get in the water during the winter up there." Tory also watches the yearly competitions on the

Tory claims, "The best ramen ever!" at Lucky Belly in Chinatown, Honolulu

North Shore, including the Eddie Aikau Big Wave Competition, which is sponsored by Quiksilver and only takes place if the wave height is high enough. She also said the Vans Triple Crown is every year. "It's pretty amazing to watch, but when the waves are good up there in the wintertime, traffic is awful. It's a two-lane highway and gets backed up fast!"

Tory also loves to *get up and go to the beach whenever* and admitted the obvious. "I love the weather. It gets chilly, 65 degrees; Ewa is always hot; [Kailua] is a little cool at night."

## DISLIKES:

Tory is enamored of the many choices of food available on the island, such as ramen, Thai, and Indian, but she still misses her favorite. "Gosh, there's everything but Mexican, and I miss it from Tucson."

The traffic is also something that Tory doesn't like but accepts. "It's a small trade-off," she admitted, but also sees a bright side. "Hawaii is trying to put in a rail from west Oahu to Honolulu." This could help ease the traffic problems according to Tory.

The expense to leave the island is also something that Tory could do without. "It's so expensive to go anywhere to take a trip . . . Europe, home . . . unless it's to the other islands."

## BEST MOMENT:

Tory reflected on her first memory of living on Oahu when she and her dad were staying at a hotel in Waikiki. "I looked out the window and saw the hustle bustle and the lights on the water. [I've] never looked back since then."

The lights of Waikiki Beach in the moonlight

## REGRETS:

Tory believes if she had researched the island prior to relocating, she would've had an easier time with housing in the beginning. "I jumped around a lot from house to house. I rushed to go elsewhere [many times]. You have to have two months' cash in your pocket because good spots go quick. There's a housing shortage."

## ADAPTATION:

Tory disclosed that it took five years to adapt to Oahu. "It's tough not knowing if you're going to be accepted, especially the first couple of years. I've heard things about the west side. I was worried about safety."

Tory admitted it's not difficult to adapt to the Hawaiian life-style. "It's easy to get on Hawaii time." She suggested that Tucson prepared her for that due to its slow-paced lifestyle. However, Tory said she stays focused because her line of work is fast paced. "I am accountable to deadlines." Because of this, living the laid-back life-style only happens for Tory outside of the workplace.

## BEST ADVICE:

Tory offered the following advice, listed below, to others who would like to relocate.

- There are lots of illegal rentals; you have to be ready to move.

- Have extra cash.

- A Costco membership is a must!

- Try to absorb the culture through activities.

- Try to meet people by joining groups.

- Don't be discouraged by roaches, ants, and bugs in your kitchen; it's part of living on an island.

- Put roach bait out.

- Living on an upper level makes no difference with bugs.

- Keep food put away.

## VERDICT:

Tory contemplated an eventual move from Oahu. "I don't think I will ever move. It'd have to be something pretty big to take me away."

A lost and found sign at Lanikai Beach in Kailua

Louise believes the only safe place to kayak on the North Shore in the winter is Anini Beach, because it has a reef protecting the shoreline

Louise and Steve

# CASE #33234: NEW LIFE FOR NEWLYWEDS

**Perpetrator(s):** Louise (58), Steve (59)
**Accomplice(s):** Dog Freya
**Time In Hawaii:** 1.5 Years
**Island:** Kauai

## BACKGROUND:

Living hectic lives in northern California, newlyweds Louise and Steve knew they wanted to start moving toward a more quiet, laid-back, and balanced lifestyle. The fast pace of their jobs in the technology industry dominated their lives. Although they were able to carve out time for golf here and there, it wasn't enough. They began thinking seriously about retiring to the central California coast.

When Louise and Steve visited Kauai and Maui a few years earlier, the islands weren't even a consideration for their retirement because of the distance from their family and friends. Their intention was to be within a few hours of San Francisco, but after finding an area further south in California that they liked, they calculated the distance to San Francisco and realized they could fly to Hawaii in the same amount of time it would take to drive to San Francisco! That joke led to serious consideration of a possible move to Hawaii.

Though Kauai felt like *a bit of a fantasy,* it also seemed like more than a vacation. It felt like home. They both asked *why not* and scheduled a trip to Kauai to meet with a real estate agent. Within six months, they owned a home on the island of Kauai; and three months after that, they moved in, with Steve arriving one week earlier than Louise.

## FINANCES:

Since Steve and Louise had begun planning seriously for retirement three years prior to their move to Kauai, there were no last-minute savings plans needed to facilitate the move. One of the things that made their funds easier to access was the immediate opening of a bank account in Hawaii; in addition, they maintained their bank account in California. They continued to use their financial advisor and tax preparer in California to avoid having problems.

## TRAVEL AND SHIPPING:

When Steve moved from the United Kingdom to California a few years prior to the Hawaii move, he used Interdean Interconex (http://www.interconex.com/) and felt they did a *good job.* Consequently, it was a simple choice when it came to choosing a mover again. Louise said, "They are more like coordinators. They were more expensive, but it gave us security." Steve and Louise packed a 14-foot container of belongings to ship but had to sell and donate a lot of their possessions. "We thinned down considerably," she said.

Louise and Steve shipped two vehicles from Oakland, California, to Kauai via Matson for about $1000 each. According to Matson (http://www.matson.com/), it takes an average of 17 days from vessel sail date to arrival at Nawiliwili because the ship goes to Honolulu first. "We sent one car in advance and kept our second car with us for the final weeks in California. The first car arrived earlier than we expected, a few days before Steve got there. I delivered our second car to Oakland the day before I left; then a friend took me to the airport the following day.

Steve and Louise's dog Freya was transported in the cargo area on the same flight Louise was on, and she said this isn't always possible. "We all flew Alaska Airlines, which I highly recommend. They are generally good for dogs; sensi-

Louise spending time at the beach with Freya

tive to pets." Upon arrival, Freya was directly released to the Humane Society (http://www.kauaihumane.org/) so she could be checked out and licensed prior to being directly released. "We had to book in advance and follow the rules absolutely to the letter. Blood tests were sent to the Department of Agriculture. The veterinarian certification had to be completed within two weeks of arrival." Louise advised that the Humane Society direct release fee was $450 for one pet and less for subsequent and returning pets. Alaska Airline charged $100 for the dog transport. "You need to plan for pets well in advance. You have to deal with paperwork, vaccinations, blood tests, and then await [the] Department of Agriculture approval. Once the blood test is submitted and approved, it's another three months before a dog is valid for entry and direct release. The test remains valid for three years, so there's no harm in doing it well in advance."

## EMPLOYMENT:

Although Louise retired prior to leaving the mainland, Steve was still working. His company agreed to let him work part-time from afar for six months, and this was acceptable to Steve. He had been hoping to retire by that time anyway.

Louise volunteers at the Kilauea Point National Wildlife Refuge, and this includes the Kilauea Point Lighthouse and walking through taro fields to locate sick birds. "They rely on volunteers as docents to share with the public." She is happy not to need a paying job!

## HOUSING:

Steve and Louise purchased a home in Princeville, close to the bluff on the North Shore of Kauai, during their last vacation to the island. They chose Princeville because it's a *lovely community* and because there's a *strong sense of community*. "The area was built as a mixed vacation resort area in the 1970s. Now, over time, it's more residential. There are lots of condos, and about half of [the people on] our street are full-time residents. It's a very pleasant neighborhood." Louise stated that it's very easy to make friends. With the mixture of families, retirees, long-term renters, and children, everyone can connect.

Louise is happy she and Steve are not on the South Shore. "The North Shore has more community . . . a more stable community . . . [and is] less vacation-oriented; [the North Shore is] more tropical with more rain." Louise also finds relief in knowing that Princeville is in a tsunami-free zone and stated, "This is where people go when there's a tsunami warning."

Home maintenance is a little different in Hawaii according to Louise. "Termites are prevalent in Hawaii. We had to *tent* our house, and you have to do it more often [than in California]. The humidity and heat makes everything rust and break more easily. You have to stay on top of it. The same goes for yard work." (*Tent* fumigation or "*tenting*" is when a tent is placed over an entire house while pesticides are being released into the vacant residence to kill any pest infestation. The sealed tent prevents the gases from escaping into the neighborhood.)

## SCHOOLING:

Louise had to become certified in CPR to work at the refuge, and the training was provided directly through Kilauea Point National Wildlife Refuge.

## ACTIVITIES:

Louise and Steve golf often, usually playing at the Makai Golf Course and sometimes at the Wailua Municipal Golf Course. Louise claimed, "[They're] not as challenging as the Prince Golf Course in Princeville." They also occasionally play at the Puakea Golf Course at an *attractive cost*, and also at the Kauai Lagoons Golf Club, both of which are located on the southern part of the island. "We avoid the South Shore because we are gone too long for the dog to be left alone." The Makai also has tennis courts, but Louise loves the tennis courts at the Hanalei Bay Resort. "Eighteen months ago, new management took over. They built up the membership. It's a thriving club with coaching and drop-ins."

Louise at an event for the refuge

Steve and Louise have kayaks and often take them to the Hanalei River. However, in the winter the only safe place to kayak on the North Shore is Anini Beach because it has a reef protecting the shoreline. They also paddle board, but only in Hanalei Bay because the river water is *too dirty*,

Steve at Kenomene overlook in Princeville

and Louise claims there are bacteria in the water. "There's a danger of leptospirosis, and it's definitely not recommended to go in the river if you have any open wounds that might get infected!" They both like Ke'e Beach on the North Shore, but dogs are not allowed there. She warned, "The county parks where there are facilities . . . no dogs are allowed in that park area."

Snorkeling is not one of Steve and Louise's favorite activities. However, they claim that Anini Beach and Tunnels Beach are the best North Shore spots to snorkel. They have also snorkeled on the South Shore at Poipu Beach Park. Louise calls this a *super area* with ". . . a little reef close to the beach with lots of fish in the winter." Most of the time she and Steve frequent Anini Beach because it's calm, but dogs are not allowed so they also frequent the Pine Trees on Hanalei Bay also known as Waioli Beach Park. Louise advised that although it's a county park, dogs are allowed on the beach with a leash; if a dog owner is caught without one, there is a hefty fine.

## SOCIALIZATION AND INTEGRATION:

Louise insists that participating in activities is the way to meet others on the island. Steve joined a men's golf group for friendly competition; Louise attends the neighborhood community meetings each month, and she visits the library for their book sales. "We come across a lot of people. If you don't belong to things, you are less likely to integrate. There are a number of clubs on the island that are very family oriented." One of those clubs is the Hanalei Canoe Club, which Louise belongs to. "[They are] dedicated to preserving the Hawaiian culture and feelings of aloha and ohana. It's a large club, and there are also a lot of mainlanders who are members. Even snowbirds join us just for a few months a year whenever they're on the island. It's a very welcoming club to all-comers and all ages. Kids 10+ are trained [to paddle] and taught about Hawaiian culture."

## HELPFUL RESOURCES:

Prior to relocating, Louise and Steve received a recommendation for a realtor on Kauai, Coreen Sarabia with Kauai Realty, Inc. (http://www.kauaipropertysource.com/). Louise revealed, "She was superb . . . did an awesome job, particularly since we were not familiar with Hawaii state regulations. She advised us well, and handled some tricky negotiations for us. We are still in touch with her from time to time. She's a delightful character. [She] went the extra mile to find an appropriate home."

Louise confessed that they were never into Internet ordering when she and Steve lived in California, but she claims Kauai is very different. "There is no choice or variety; we order a lot online and get things shipped." Steve and Louise have taken advantage of Amazon's free shipping service, called Amazon Prime, so they try to order through this service prior to looking elsewhere unless prices are much lower somewhere else.

Although Louise and Steve didn't end up having to rent a car on the island, she did research prior to arriving in case they needed to rent a vehicle. "We had great success with Discount Hawaii Car Rental (http://discounthawaiicarrental.com/). We were able to find great rates, and they simply work through all the regular car companies, so you just get treated as a regular customer. There's no cancellation fee so no risk."

Louise used the Hawaii Department of Agriculture website (http://hdoa.hawaii.gov/) to obtain updated information on importing animals.

For local product information, Louise suggests visiting a website that helps support the usage of Kauai-made products (http://www.kauaimade.net/).

The outrigger canoe club that Louise belongs to is the Hanalei Canoe Club (http://hanaleicanoeclub.org/).

## LIKES:

Louise loves the weather and said, "It goes hand in hand with the extra time we have now," so they can enjoy more outdoor activities. They hike occasionally when visitors come to see them, and they like walking the dog on the beaches and through their neighborhood. "To be close to the ocean was important. The birds are amazing; the scenery is amazing."

Louise also likes Kauai for its rural feel and because it's not overbuilt. "The Hawaiians are against corporations." This prevents excessive building on the island.

## DISLIKES:

Quite adamantly, Louise proclaimed she dislikes, "CENTIPEDES! COCKROACHES! MOSQUITOES!" But not much else bothers her. Louise and Steve have Mokihana Pest Control, Inc. exterminate the perimeter of their house to prevent pests from entering and said, "They do a good job . . . not only against centipedes but also ants, spiders, etc."

Louise offered the proper way to deal with centipedes. "Pick them up with kitchen tongs (not fingers), and chuck them down the waste disposal." Neither Louise nor Steve has been bitten by a centipede, but she keeps meat tenderizer in the refrigerator just in case, which has been known to help with the pain.

She hasn't experienced *island fever*, a claustrophobic feeling of being trapped, and has no desire to leave the island. She did leave for a short burst once to visit the Big Island in support of a leukemia organization and again to visit Oahu to pick out granite for their kitchen. "I was totally excited to get back to Kauai!"

Louise admits she does spend her life on Kauai cleaning, since the doors and windows are open all of the time. With the dampness also comes mold, which she combats with a special cleaning solution. "I've used Method grapefruit cleaner and Windex, but I started using GreenMaxPro a few months ago, which is available at several places, including farmers' markets and some pharmacies. I buy the concentrate at North Shore Pharmacy in Kilauea and dilute it myself." Louise has also tried coconut oil for leather but warned it left spots. "Don't bring leather. It gets moldy. You'll clean it every five minutes."

> "Don't bring leather. It gets moldy. You'll clean it every five minutes."

## BEST MOMENT:

Louise knew right from the start that she and Steve made the right choice. "It feels like home. A day doesn't go by that I don't say *I can't believe I'm here.* It's amazing. I love life here."

## REGRETS:

Any regrets were circumvented with Louise and Steve's research, which prevented some mistakes like quarantining their dog. She is also glad that they paid extra for movers to give them peace of mind during the relocation.

## ADAPTATION:

Since Louise and Steve chose to live in an area populated mainly by people from the mainland, they haven't become integrated into the local Hawaiian community to any extent. Therefore, they adapted to Kauai fairly easily. "If we lived in Wailua Homesteads or Kapaa, we would integrate more," Louise presumed, and added that Hawaiians keep to themselves.

Because of Louise's participation in outrigger canoeing, she is experiencing the culture to a certain degree by befriending families, both Hawaiian and transplants.

## BEST ADVICE:

Louise offered some advice, listed below, for others wanting to relocate to Hawaii. In addition, she thinks others can get some good information on her own blog (http://www.kauaigreenhorn.com/). "It's not really intended as a guide to folks who might want to move here, but you might pick up some stuff from the early posts."

- Quarantining your pet is not required—do research about direct release.

- Spend one to two weeks as a local: eating, shopping, and participating in activities.

- A detailed project plan is a must.

- Seriously consider whether or not you can be away from your family—some only survive a few months away.

- If you need culture like art, theater, and movies, you're not going to be happy on Kauai.

- Shopoholics will not do well on Kauai.

- Be comfortable with living like you're in a foreign country.

## VERDICT:

"We have no finite plans [to leave]," insists Louise. "We are here for as long as our bodies allow us to be here. If we need heavier medical maintenance or can't drive . . . that's why we'd go."

Tanya and her family frequent Ko'Olina Beach where the new Disney Hotel is located. "Ko'Olina is great for kids. The breaks are not hard. It's safe and protected," she said.

Tanya and Jeremiah

## CASE #39746: ON A WING AND A PRAYER

**Perpetrator(s):** Tanya (39), Jeremiah (35)
**Accomplice(s):** Son (5), Daughter (3)
**Time In Hawaii:** 3.5 Years
**Island:** Oahu

## BACKGROUND:

Newly married, Tanya and Jeremiah each had a child from a previous marriage. Their blended family soon grew as Tanya and Jeremiah had a baby together. They both had good jobs in northern California and were *living an everyday normal life.* With Jeremiah's son living with his mother and after Tanya's son left home to attend the University of Hawaii at Manoa, the talks became serious about a relocation to southern California or Hawaii.

"Everyone thought we were joking," explained Tanya. "But then we started planning. We kept talking about the move to keep us going."

Jeremiah and Tanya were not strangers to Hawaii. Jeremiah had attended college at Hawaii Pacific University on Oahu and stayed on the island two years thereafter until returning to California to pursue his career. Tanya spent time on Oahu and Kauai, once to run the Honolulu Marathon, and another time to vacation with the family. Now with Tanya's son attending college on Oahu, the choice was easily made.

Tanya shared, "We buckled down, saved some money, moved into my mom's house for four months to wrap up everything." With a young child still at home and a baby on the way, two years later Tanya and Jeremiah purchased three one-way tickets to Oahu on a direct flight from San Jose.

## FINANCES:

Tanya and Jeremiah saved diligently for six months prior to their move to Oahu. "We could've used a little extra [money] . . . to open up our own business." They are aiming at saving enough to open a food truck within the next year.

## TRAVEL AND SHIPPING:

To make the move to Oahu easier, Tanya and Jeremiah sold everything except their clothes, pictures, and some other personal items. They shipped 30 boxes via express shipping to the address of a friend who already lived on Oahu. They received a huge shipping discount because Tanya's brother-in-law worked for the company. The boxes were shipped and received in three days for a mere $1600. One vehicle was shipped using Matson (http://www.matson.com/), at a cost of about $1000, and it took two to three weeks for it to arrive.

## EMPLOYMENT:

Jeremiah worked for a major grocery chain in California and was promised a transfer to Oahu, which was one of the main reasons for choosing that island. However, three weeks prior to the family's move, the company had a change of heart and rescinded their offer of employment. Needing to make a decision quickly, Jeremiah and Tanya decided to follow through on their plans to move to Oahu. "On a wing and a prayer, we made the decision [to move] and to see where it takes us," Tanya confessed.

> "On a wing and a prayer, we made the decision [to move] and to see where it takes us," Tanya confessed.

Since the baby was due soon after the family arrived in Hawaii, the plan was for Tanya to take a year off of work. In order to accommodate this plan, Jeremiah quickly found a construction job on the island with a company that, to his surprise, was owned by his distant cousin! When the baby arrived, Jeremiah was able to take a couple of months off to spend time with the family.

When the baby was eight months old, Tanya began looking for work and decided to pursue licensure to sell insurance. She felt this type of job would be flexible enough to enable her to tend to the needs of her family. She is now a full-time insurance representative but is often able to work out of her home office.

## HOUSING:

When Tanya and Jeremiah arrived on Oahu, they were lucky to already have an acquaintance in Ewa Beach who could accommodate their family for four months until they found a permanent place to live. "Regardless of them letting us stay to transition from California, we would've still moved here, but just would've done things differently. We would've had a place prior to moving here, and I probably would've had my daughter [delivered] in California. Nonetheless, we would've still moved here."

After arriving on Oahu, Tanya and Jeremiah pursued their own housing by searching Craigslist, and they secured a rental property four months later in the West Loch Community of Ewa Beach. They rented a one-bedroom apartment in an eight-plex building for $1200 per month. Tanya explained, "West Loch is a beautiful area with single family homes, duplexes, and eight-plexes. It's tree lined and absolutely beautiful. There are always people outside and it's a nice place to raise a family. There is not much in the way of community events here. The reason we stayed so long [in the one-bedroom apartment] is because the owner lives around the corner and pays utilities except gas and electric. She's a super nice lady," Tanya explained.

Recently, Tanya and her family moved into a four-bedroom duplex in Ewa Beach at the Waterfront at Pu'uloa, a housing community that is an old military base but is now open to civilians. Jeremiah found out about it through his co-workers. "We LOVE, LOVE, LOVE living there!" Tanya affirmed. She is excited that the new neighborhood has events, including farmers' markets and movie nights on the beach. She is ecstatic that the beach is in her own backyard! She is also happy that the area has a strong sense of community.

## SCHOOLING:

Tanya pursued licensing on her own and without a sponsor in order to sell accident and health insurance. She took the exam at a local company that proctored it.

Tanya stated, "Hawaii is big on private schools. High school admittance is easier if [already attending] a private school [for elementary and middle school]." She claimed that the private schools are very expensive, with tuition for a two year old around $2400 per month. Tanya and Jeremiah's son attends kindergarten at the local public school and *loves* it! Their daughter attends preschool. "The public schools do not allow a child [under] five to go to kindergarten if born [after the deadline]."

This was different than when her son started kindergarten at four and a half years old. Tanya and Jeremiah's son's school is year round and is also known as a *track school*. "There are four quarters with a three-week break each quarter." Previously the school didn't offer before- and after-school care. However, that has recently changed. "The YMCA just started intercession care." This provides the students with before- and after-school care, which will help ease the burden for families.

> Tanya stated, "Hawaii is big on private schools. High school admittance is easier if [already attending] a private school [for elementary and middle school]."

## ACTIVITIES:

Jeremiah and Tanya often visit beaches and seek areas that don't have big waves so their children can swim and boogie board. "We mostly go to Iroquois Point Beach down the street in Ewa Beach," Tanya offered. They also frequent Magic Island in Waikiki and Ko'Olina near Waianae. This is where the new Disney Hotel is located. "Ko'Olina is great for kids. The breaks are not hard. It's safe and protected." Ko'Olina is also where their children feel comfortable snorkeling.

Tanya would like to hike more, but until she and Jeremiah's newest addition to the family, a daughter, is older, they are limited on the hikes they can do. "We went to Maniloni Falls . . . a medium hike . . . [and] it was too hard with a child in the backpack." According to Tanya, the Aiea Loop Trail and Maakapu'u Point Lighthouse Trail (which is paved) are much easier hikes with children.

The Pearl Harbor Bike Path is a trail that Tanya and Jeremiah have biked. Though it used to be maintained by the state, it isn't any longer. "But people still use the path," Tanya said.

## SOCIALIZATION AND INTEGRATION:

Recently Jeremiah and Tanya joined a running group called Spartan Race, (http://www.spartanrace.com/). They work out with this group by competing in obstacle courses and train with one of the teams at Patsy T. Mink Central Oahu Regional Park in the Waipio area. "It's really involved. It's a social workout group . . . and kids go [with their parents]." Tanya is especially excited that, between the two of them, she and Jeremiah have lost a total of 48 pounds!

When they arrived on Oahu, Tanya and Jeremiah already knew a few people on the island, and they have since met many others through her job. "We put ourselves out there. We're social."

## HELPFUL RESOURCES:

Tanya used Zillow (http://www.zillow.com/) and Craigslist when looking for housing. She and Jeremiah also drove around looking for rental properties. Since they arrived on Oahu without any furniture, they shopped Sears and JC Penney at first but ended up finding some good deals at local mom-and-pop stores. "We took our time and shopped around. We wanted to save money. It took a few months to get everything."

Tanya and Jeremiah's newest addition to their family was born at Kaiser Permanente Moanalua Medical Center, also called Kaiser Red Hill. Tanya enjoyed the birthing experience and stated, "The staff was awesome! I had no problems there and they took good care of me and my baby. They are definitely a great facility. The staff was easy to work with. Definitely a wonderful experience that makes me smile when I think back to that day!"

## LIKES:

Tanya and Jeremiah love the weather but explained *that's a given.* "Any time we can go to the beach, and it's always beautiful."

Tanya loves the Hawaiian motto *God first and family first,* with everything else being secondary and has witnessed that in action by Jeremiah's employer. "If the kids get sick, they say *go handle your family.* There are no guilt trips if we're sick or have to stay home." Her husband can easily take off work if the family needs his help.

Tanya is also a fan of the soulful food on the island. "The cuisine is awesome. Food is probably one of the more expensive things. To me it's worth it to pay a little extra."

## DISLIKES:

For a long time, Tanya struggled with having her baby away from her family. "I was homesick at first but got past it. It took about six months. I was so sad at first." Tanya explains that, because of technology, she is able to connect regularly with her family on the mainland. "FaceTime, Skype, Facebook . . . they all played a big part for my family to see my kids grow up. We do birthday parties on FaceTime."

Tanya wishes connecting with local Hawaiians was easier. "If you're not local, you have to build a relationship. It takes a while to build trust. Then you'll be like family. You become truly ohana, and it makes you feel good."

## BEST MOMENT:

Every time Tanya is outdoors with her family, she is reminded of the reason they moved to Oahu. "With the kids at the beach, always outdoors, you don't need a lot. Simplicity . . . it's very simple. We were looking to be happy in a simple way. You don't need all the bells and whistles."

## REGRETS:

Even though the relocation was difficult at first, Tanya does not regret moving to Oahu. "Not having my daughter born back home for all to see is hard." She also wished she'd done a better job sorting through all of the family's belongings. "It's hard to let go of things. I constantly had to ask myself *Why did I send this over?*" After unpacking, she realized that at least five entire boxes could have been thrown away, which would have saved them more money.

## ADAPTATION:

Tanya and Jeremiah try every day to experience Hawaii. They try to be involved at the schools and try to embrace the island culture. The culture is what made them stay. "It's very different on other islands. Oahu is busy . . . a hustle bustle . . . but the west side is slower. It's a wonderful island culture. It's such a great place to raise kids. We are always looking for new things and meeting people."

Originally, Jeremiah and Tanya decided it would help them adjust if they could return to their hometown for a visit every January, but that didn't happen. Instead, they have become each other's source of comfort. "The family spends a lot of time together. We have been rocks for each other, which is huge. It makes the day-to-day easier."

## BEST ADVICE:

Tanya's simple advice listed below is geared toward avoiding making a mistake.

- ◆ Plan.

- ◆ Save enough money *just in case.*

- ◆ Expect unexpected expenses.

- ◆ You can't wing it—you can't drive home if it doesn't work.

## VERDICT:

Jeremiah and Tanya were going to give Oahu a chance until their son started kindergarten and then decide whether or not they would stay, but that was over six months ago! "We're here to stay." Tanya admitted that she doesn't know where life will take them. "[My] son is 22 and will be graduating this year. When I have grandbabies, I don't know how I'll feel. We want to plant roots here." However, Tanya maintained that they will never oppose what life hands them.

Eric picked a fresh papaya from a tree in his back yard that was the size of a football! "I took it inside, washed it off, cut it in half, and ate the whole thing in one sitting. It was so *ono!*"

Caren and Eric

# CASE #16124: THE LONG WAY AROUND THE WORLD

**Perpetrator(s):** Caren (37), Eric (40)
**Accomplice(s):** None
**Time In Hawaii:** 7 Months
**Island:** Maui

## BACKGROUND:

She didn't know it then, but while traveling throughout Europe in high school, and then again later by herself, Caren was preparing for another cultural experience: moving to Hawaii. With nearly a dozen trips to the Hawaiian Islands under her belt, first as a competitor on a cheerleading squad and multiple times later for vacations, Caren's love for Kauai had her dreaming about relocating to the island from Austin, Texas.

Formerly working as a nanny for a popular country band, Caren realized she wasn't happy. After posting an ad on Craigslist for a snowboarding buddy, Eric came into the picture. He had spent his life outdoors, camping and exploring nature in Portland, Oregon, and had traveled to Canada and Mexico. After moving to Austin,

Texas, to study audio engineering, he soon realized that profession wasn't his calling in life, so he made a switch to selling motorcycles, one of his passions. Caren opened his eyes to the world of traveling.

Caren's career in massage therapy was flourishing in Texas, so she simply asked her global employer for a transfer to Hawaii. She soon had the job transfer secured on the island of Kauai, so she and Eric decided to take the long way to their new home. They spent nine months traveling throughout Europe and Asia before arriving to Hawaii. Unfortunately, the job on Kauai fell through before they even arrived, but a job on Maui opened up. On a little island called Bali in Indonesia, Caren and Eric made the decision to settle on a move to Maui.

## FINANCES:

After saving nearly $43,000 between the two of them, Caren and Eric left for Europe. Although their plans were loose and formed along the way, the goal was to arrive on Maui with at least $4,000. Eric met this financial objective, but Caren arrived on Maui with only $300. She put her good credit to use and took advantage of zero percent credit card offers and lived off of these until she got on her feet. Although a debt was incurred, she is now stable enough to pay the debt off in a short amount of time. Eric recalled, "If I hadn't found work within two months, our situation would be completely different today."

Caren and Eric rented an island car, an older vehicle that blends in like a local vehicle, for about $20 a day; it was a 2005 Nissan Sentra in ill repair. Caren soon discovered that no auto loans are available on Maui. The only loans that she found were personal loans; in order to secure one, a person has to be able to verify income on the island for at least three months. But her father rescued her and spent $2000 to ship her grandmother's 1995 Toyota Camry, which was supposedly in good condition. Unfortunately when Caren received the vehicle, she discovered it was in need of a lot of work. To combat the problem, Eric purchased a motorcycle and, after many repairs, Grandma's car has progressed to good working order.

## TRAVEL AND SHIPPING:

Prior to leaving for their backpacking trip, Caren and Eric sold everything they owned on Craigslist. They had looked into shipping everything, but at a cost of $20,000, it didn't appear to be an economical choice. Instead, they decided to purchase used furniture and household goods upon arrival.

Caren and Eric purchased plane tickets from Austin to India and then to Thailand. It wasn't until they arrived in Thailand that they purchased plane tickets to Malaysia, Indonesia and finally Maui.

## EMPLOYMENT:

Upon leaving Indonesia for Maui, Caren received the phone call that had been her worst nightmare. The spa that was going to hire her decided they wanted massage therapists at the new spa to also have certification in aesthetics (skin care). Caren did not possess such a certification. "At that moment, my life fell apart," she shared. "I was bawling hysterically!" With Kauai still on her mind, she and Eric thought intensely for two weeks about redirecting their relocation to Kauai instead, but in the end, they decided to follow through with their Maui plans.

When she arrived on Maui, Caren had to decide whether to attend aesthetics school or find another massage position. She decided on aesthetics school and attended for three and a half months. At the same time, she applied for other massage positions and claimed she interviewed everywhere! She finally received an offer; however, because of the long commute, she turned it down. During this time,

Caren used credit cards to cover her living expenses. She remembered, "For a while, we really, really struggled."

Eric began applying for jobs while he and Caren were in Indoncsia. Some of those leads led to interviews once he arrived on Maui. Shortly after arrival to the island, he secured a position in cellular phone sales. His passion is to work in the solar energy industry, and he's attending school on Maui to work toward that goal. He is still employed by the same company that he worked for when they first arrived.

## HOUSING:

Caren tried to arrange housing in Maui while she was in Bali, but landlords didn't pay attention to her requests. "If you're not on-island, they don't want to talk to you; you're a waste of their time because so many people dream of being here so they try to line it up in advance." Caren added that landlords don't have the time to field every dreamer's inquiry. Because of this, Caren made reservations at a hotel in Wailuku for three nights to allow time to search for housing upon arrival.

> Caren explained, "It is so difficult to find a rental. It's not good enough to have a job and references. There are 100+ applicants for each rental."

Caren explained, "It is so difficult to find a rental. It's not good enough to have a job and references. There are 100+ applicants for each rental." That's why when Caren found a rental listing for a short-term, fully furnished ohana in Wailuku for $1100 a month including utilities, she and Eric called the landlord immediately upon landing at the airport. Luckily, they secured the housing and moved into the ohana within a couple days. "I did love the view from our kitchen window in Wailuku . . . of Iao Valley . . . it's so beautiful.

I also loved seeing the view of the mountains while driving home in that direction."

Needing to relocate because the short-term lease was due to expire, Eric and Caren decided to focus their search in Wailea in South Maui to shorten their commute to work and to experience *sunnier weather*. Caren worked tirelessly to find suitable housing at an affordable price. It wasn't until her parents visited from the mainland that she got a break. "My parents were in a VRBO that had an attached ohana

> Caren worked tirelessly to find suitable housing at an affordable price.

that was under construction and would soon be available to rent. My mom called me and told me she found a place for me." (VRBO means Vacation Rental By Owner.) Caren immediately went to check out the property in Wailea and confirmed it was *gorgeous with an ocean view*. She fell in love with it and decided to rent the two-bedroom ohana for $2,000/month. Although it was over their budget, Caren said if she and Eric didn't use their air conditioning, they would be able to afford it.

Caren loves Wailea and said, "It is upscale with quiet, older people. There are no roosters or barking dogs, which is very different than Wailuku."

## SCHOOLING:

Both Caren and Eric attended school on Maui. Upon arrival, Caren had to decide whether to obtain her aesthetics certification or find a different massage job that didn't require it. After talking with her mom, she decided to attend a three-and-a-half month certification program at Spa Luna, an aesthetics school. The cost was around $7000 and, surprisingly, her mother paid for it! Caren loved the school and said, "It was laid back [without] a lot of rules. Very Hawaiian style."

Most of the students had lived on the island their whole lives and few were from elsewhere.

Although Eric gained employment immediately, he still decided to pursue school. He enrolled at Solar Energy International (http://www .solarenergy.org/) to obtain a Residential and Commercial Photovoltaic Systems Certificate. The program cost $3200 and is 19 weeks long. The school allows the classes to be arranged around work schedules.

## ACTIVITIES:

After seven months on Maui, Caren and Eric went on a hike in upcountry Maui called Waihou Springs Trail off of Olinda Road. "It was nice to get a break from the heat in Kihei and chaos in Kahului and hike into the cool and shady pine forest and eucalyptus trees.

Caren and Eric in Iao Valley

We were only 20 minutes from Kahului, but it felt like we were in another land," she shared.

Eric and Caren also spent some time visiting the town of Lahaina. Prior to that, the last recreational time they had shared was a visit to Kapalua Beach in West Maui near Napili. "It is gorgeous over there and we could see Molokai, Lanai, and Oahu from there," Caren recalled.

With five long days at work and then running errands on the weekends, they don't have much time to enjoy the island the way they'd like to. Eric said it well: "My work-life balance right now is not good. It's 99 percent work and one percent life, but that one percent is quality; we're on Maui after all."

## SOCIALIZATION AND INTEGRATION:

Caren has met most of her friends through aesthetics school and at her current massage job, and she finds the locals to be friendly. "Being well-traveled, I am ultra-sensitive to other cultures. I go the extra mile to not infringe," she shared. "And after learning about [Hawaii's] history, it made sense. As long as you don't make fun of local people and their ways, you'll be fine."

Eric contributed, "I work so many hours a week, I don't have the time or energy to do anything [else]; I work 10 to 11 hours a day and it just drains me." Eric does see himself being able to volunteer for good causes eventually and hopes to change jobs soon to enable him to do that.

## HELPFUL RESOURCES:

Although Caren said that Craigslist is the only source she uses to buy items, she admits, "Dealing with Craigslist to get items is difficult. An old couch that would cost $100 in Texas is $500 on Maui, and it's something I wouldn't even want to lay my head on." Because of these types of difficulties, Caren and Eric slept on an air mattress for months. According to Caren, sellers on Craigslist don't return calls. "They are not flexible. They make huge demands and then are no-shows."

Eric confessed to searching for any website or blog that focused on moving to Hawaii. His curiosity with Craigslist helped him to understand the cost of items for his future arrival to the island.

## LIKES:

Eric likes the fact that the people on Maui are courteous and friendly, and that no one seems to be in a hurry. He attributes this to the *small town* mentality of the island. He enjoys the availability of fresh papaya and lilikoi (passion fruit) in his own backyard and claims that the ocean *soothes the soul.* Eric is amazed at the night sky in Maui. "The stars are so incredible at night. We can see distant galaxies with the naked eye!"

Caren especially loves the beauty of Maui. "It's so nice to live somewhere where the scenery takes your breath away." She also enjoys and honors the Hawaiian culture and its traditions. "Coming from Texas where the main traditions are barbecue and football, the Hawaiian connections to nature and its spirits are truly mesmerizing."

Caren was surprised at one aspect of nature on Maui—geckos. "I also wasn't expecting to adopt geckos as friends or pets. The Madagascar Gecko is gorgeous, and we've even named one of them that lives near our kitchen window Stubbs."

## DISLIKES:

Caren was shocked to find that the only stores available for shopping were Walmart, Kmart, Ross, Macy's, and the Salvation Army, and Eric was disappointed that there wasn't an Apple Store nearby. Shopping resale stores in Maui results in rusted silverware and *gross* clothing, Caren shared.

Eric misses the mountains and snow he had access to on the mainland. "I feel really disconnected from the land having no distinct seasons during the year in Hawaii. I grew up in Oregon and came to love the four seasons. It's 80 degrees here every day; every day feels the same, and time blasts by so fast."

Another long-term concern of Eric's is the cost of living on Maui. "I can't imagine paying the super inflated rent prices here for any longer than a year. I would want to buy a condo or small home if we plan to stay here five years." Eric admitted that purchasing a property where he and Caren can have their own private, spacious place would come at a very high price.

Caren and Eric have many little concerns listed below, and the sum total of these might determine how long they stay on Maui.

- No nightlife

- Very limited live music

- Very few choices of affordable ethnic cuisine

- Excessive amount of bugs, from roaches to gnats to centipedes

- High prices of food, even with a local discount

- Relentless sugar cane burning

- Open air testing of pesticides and herbicides

- Lack of responses to emails

- High sales taxes

## BEST MOMENT:

Despite the negatives of the island, both Eric and Caren are in awe of Maui's landscape. They both enjoy exploring Maui together just like tourists. That helps remind Caren why she is on the island, along with regularly taking notes when nature inspires her. "The other day while giving a massage at the spa, I saw whales from the window. It was so amazing!"

With a crowd of people on New Year's Eve, Eric and Caren watched the last sunset of the year from Haleakala. It was then that Eric realized, "We live here now; they all have to go home." His amazement didn't end that night. "[I picked] a fresh papaya from our back yard that was the size of a football! I took it inside, washed it off, cut it in half, and ate the whole thing in one sitting. It was so *ono!*" (*Ono* is a Hawaiian word meaning absolutely delicious.)

## REGRETS:

Caren's only regret was that she didn't bring her Subaru with her to Maui. "It would've only cost $2000 to ship." Trying to find a used vehicle upon arrival posed some problems. "Used vehicles here are super expensive. [They're] rusted, barely running, and 30 to 40 percent higher [priced] than on the mainland. I thought more would be available."

Eric's regret is leaving his cat behind. "Although my parents are taking care of her, I really wish I could get her here with me. She's an elderly cat, and sending her here would likely kill her. I desperately want to go back to visit her before she dies."

## ADAPTATION:

Caren and Eric insist that understanding the history of Hawaii and its culture is imperative to living the lifestyle in a way that doesn't disrespect the Hawaiians. "It's basically living with aloha, considering others before yourself. It's doing the right thing."

Caren thinks she and Eric are still adjusting to the culture change and "don't quite feel settled yet." He believes they have at least adjusted to the daily routine of life on Maui. "We don't honk our horn. We always let people walk across the street in front of our vehicles, or let other cars turn or merge in front of us when there's traffic." Eric maintains that he respects the Hawaiian culture a lot and thinks the world could learn a great deal from the Hawaiian people.

Besides the occasional haole joke, Eric said that the Hawaiians are very accepting and that the term "haole" can simply mean that someone is new to the island. However, he suggested this term can also be used when referring to a newcomer who is disrespecting the land, people, or culture. "It can be a joke if you're cool or an insult if you're ignorant."

## BEST ADVICE:

Eric and Caren warn that Maui will test you. "The island will either accept you or chew you up and spit you out," Eric related. "I've met a lot of people who have told me if you aren't doing what you're supposed to be doing here, the island will fight you." He has witnessed people falling into this category. "It's just a mysterious force at times that you have no control over." Eric maintains that it depends on how much you want to be in Hawaii and what challenges you are willing to go through to stay.

Caren and Eric offer some advice that may help others transition to Hawaii without any surprises.

- Come with as much money as possible.

- Ship a car and anything else that is important to you.

- Search immediately upon arrival for furnished property with short-term leases; it's a great way to get started and find your way.

- Don't expect to be able to have a job or housing lined up in advance.

- Don't expect to maintain the same lifestyle you had on the mainland.

- Invest in a Costco membership; it's worth it just for the cheaper gas.

- Be considerate and understanding of the local culture.

- Be an observer for a while; don't make waves or disrespect anyone.

- Be open to part-time jobs.

- When driving, slow down, stop speeding, and don't use your horn.

- Relax.

- Plan on cooking every day due to the expense of eating out.

- To better understand the Hawaiian culture, learn the correct history of how and why the U.S. took ownership of the Hawaiian Islands.

- Be ready to face challenges and to find out who you really are.

## VERDICT:

Caren would love to stay but said she doesn't know if the level of difficulty to live on the island is worth the benefits. "I was really hoping to raise a family here, but I don't want to raise [children] at [the] poverty level. Being here is like being on a roller coaster. There are really good days when I'm excited and feel like anything is possible; then there are bad days where I feel bad for dragging Eric here and contemplate where we would go next."

Eric claims he wasn't dragged to Maui at all. "I jumped at the idea to travel around the world for eight months with the woman I love and see if we could build a life here in Hawaii. I think it will take at least a year for us to know what living here is really like and if we want to stay."

Both Jennafer and Jenna have snorkeled at Lanikai Beach on the east side of the island, and Jennafer claimed it is not the best place to snorkel. "The water can be mucky if the winds are blowing."

From left to right: Jenna and Jennafer

## CASE #33451: SMART MOVE

**Perpetrator(s):** Jennafer (28), Jenna (26)
**Accomplice(s):** Dog Sam (17 Lbs.)
**Time In Hawaii:** 5 Months
**Island:** Oahu

. . . . . . . . . . . . . . . . . . . . . . . . . . . . . . . . . . . . . . . . . . . . . . . . . . . . . . .

## BACKGROUND:

Both Jennafer and Jenna obtained their undergraduate degrees in psychology, but it wasn't until graduate school that they met. "I have a passion toward people and science," Jennafer shared. It was only a coincidence that they shared the same degree. Jenna has a similar desire to help others and is an Emergency Medical Technician (EMT).

Jennafer grew up on a farm in Northern Illinois "with horses, chickens . . . a small town." She admits she had a *very outdoorsy, adventurous childhood*, which perhaps fueled her interest in the outdoor lifestyle of Hawaii. Jenna, on the other hand, grew up close to Chicago, Illinois, but said she was still an *outdoor girl*. "From as early as I can remember, my mom always made sure I spent at least two hours a day outside. As long as I was active, I was happy," Jenna said. Both resided in Chicago immediately prior to their relocation to Hawaii.

209

Jennafer was happy in Chicago. She was finishing up her doctoral studies in psychology and was looking forward to a year-long residency before becoming a licensed psychologist. Jenna, the free spirit of the two, had different ideas . . . one being a relocation to Oahu. They went to Oahu shortly before their relocation and *fell in love* with the island. "I started applying for fellowships at that point," Jennafer said. Although she was happy to have been accepted into a residency program on Oahu, it was a tough decision to pick up and move. "Jenna wanted to move. I am more conservative."

Jennafer revealed that three days after her graduation, she and Jenna ". . . packed up our whole lives in six heavy suitcases," and left for Hawaii.

## FINANCES:

From the time Jennafer and Jenna first visited Hawaii, it was nine months until they relocated to Oahu. Jennafer saved all of her gift money from her recent graduation, which helped her pay to ship a few things and to place a deposit on an apartment when she and Jenna arrived on Oahu. Unfortunately, Jenna's mother had passed away a year before the move, and as a result she inherited money that she was able to use to finance her move. "We tried to split the costs evenly, but Jenna paid for most. But I'm very diligent to [continue to] save money," Jennafer said.

## TRAVEL AND SHIPPING:

Besides the six heavy suitcases, Jennafer and Jenna didn't take anything to Oahu except Jennafer's vehicle. To ship it they used C.A.R. Logistics (http://www.car-logistics.com/) and paid $1195 to ship the vehicle completely empty, which took about a week to arrive. Jennafer and Jenna drove the vehicle from Illinois to Los Angeles, California, where the vehicle was shipped from. A friend drove them from Los Angeles to San Diego, where their flight to Oahu originated.

Jennafer's mom shipped two small boxes later via standard shipping through the U.S. Postal Service for about $75 each. "Suitcases are cheaper to fly [on the plane] than shipping boxes," Jennafer shared. Due to the high expense of shipping, all of her and Jenna's furniture is still at Jenna's dad's house in Illinois.

Because Jennafer took her dog Sam to Hawaii, she spent much time researching animal transportation. She strongly suggested using Alaska Airlines. "They are dog friendly . . . lots of good reviews." Sam traveled as a service dog because Jennafer uses the dog in therapy, so he was free to transport, and was able to travel in a crate under the seat. Listed below are the different requirements and some costs she accrued to transport Sam.

- Rabies

- Immunizations

- Microchip ($100)

- Blood work ($300)

Jennafer added, ". . . it was $400 to $500 before we left." Because of the extensive preparation, Sam qualified for direct release upon arrival to Oahu. "At the airport, people took him to the quarantine station; we went straight to the office with him." Jennafer also shared that a big dog would have cost $700 to ship in cargo, which is why she and Jenna didn't take their 125-pound dog and instead left it with Jennafer's mom in Illinois.

For the first two weeks on Oahu, Jennafer and Jenna rented a vehicle at the airport for only $274. Within that same two weeks, Jenna purchased a vehicle. "She got a car loan without employment!"

Jennafer shared but thought it was because Jenna had enough of a down payment to qualify.

## EMPLOYMENT:

Jennafer started her residency in Honolulu two weeks after arrival on Oahu. "I am paid minimally. I will eventually get three times the pay when I am fully certified."

Jenna applied for jobs immediately upon arrival. "She was told not to apply until she had a Hawaii address," Jennafer said. Jenna started a job six weeks later, but unfortunately it wasn't as an EMT but as a patient care representative at a hospital. She applied for jobs directly with each hospital on the island via their websites and also searched for jobs on the website http://www.monster.com/ and Craigslist. Jennafer said, surprised, "It took her six months to get a job [as an EMT]!" Jenna eventually obtained a job as an EMT at the hospital where she was already working as a patient care representative.

Looking to the future, Jennafer is contemplating her employment possibilities. She can continue to work where she is currently fulfilling her residency requirements with a significant pay increase, or she can go back to Chicago and open a practice. "I don't want to own a practice in Hawaii," she shared, because she has more contacts and relationships in Chicago.

## HOUSING:

Jenna and Jennafer did *quite a lot* of research before moving to Oahu, but they didn't want to commit to housing without seeing properties first. They had a good idea where they wanted to live and knew they were interested in Honolulu, the Hawaii Kai area, the east side of the island, and Ewa Beach.

Quickly ruling out Honolulu because of the high prices and because they encountered a lot of trouble finding a landlord who would accept pets, Jennafer and Jenna's search took them farther away from Honolulu. "There's really limited housing for pets," Jennafer revealed. The east side of the island proved to be beyond their price range as well. They found Ewa Beach to be better priced, with more options for pets. According to Jennafer, they would have needed a budget of $3000 per month to rent a place in Honolulu compared to $1700 a month for a similar place in Ewa Beach.

Prior to leaving the mainland, Jennafer and Jenna secured temporary quarters on Oahu at two separate places for a total of 10 days through Airbnb, Inc. (https://www.airbnb.com/), a website dedicated to connecting homeowners to travelers. It includes rental options from boats to single rooms to entire houses. "It's kind of like subletting. We stayed in someone's spare bedroom in Hawaii Kai for under a $100 a night. It's like a host family," Jennafer said.

Jenna and Jennafer

"[The second place] was another room that had roughly 15 other individuals in the house. Many of the individuals live in the home permanently, whereas rooms like ours are rented out to vacationers. [It cost] $605 for seven nights," Jennafer shared.

Jenna and Jennafer looked on Craigslist for housing in Honolulu and tried to find a two-bedroom apartment so they'd have room for guests. "We already looked at five or six [apartments], but the price was too high for a two-bedroom or they were not well-kept," Jennafer said. Within a week, they found a two-bedroom condo for $1700 per month in Ewa Beach.

Jennafer likes the Ewa Beach community. "It's very well kept. It's a very beautiful subdivision . . . a beautiful townhome. The neighbors are nice. It feels safe. And it's pet friendly." They are also lucky to have air conditioning, but they only use it at night. She and Jenna's electric bill is around $105 per month. The downside of the Ewa Beach condo is that it takes Jennafer one hour to commute each way to her job. "If I leave at four-thirty, it takes me one and a half hours. If I leave at four o'clock, it's forty-five minutes. I beat the traffic."

## SCHOOLING:

Jenna has applied and been accepted to graduate school for nursing at the University of Hawaii at Manoa (http://manoa.hawaii.edu/) and at a college in Chicago at a private university. According to Jennafer, to be considered a resident at UH Manoa, you have to start school after you have worked on the island for one full year. If you miss that deadline, then you will be considered a non-resident. Jenna missed that deadline by five days! She said the tuition is $80,000 per year as a non-resident and $40,000 per year as a resident.

## ACTIVITIES:

Jennafer said what she and Jenna love most about Oahu is the choice of activities. "The quality of life makes a huge difference; [there's] hiking, cliff jumping, running. Jenna is a fun free spirit. She is trying to learn to surf at the White Plains Beach [in Ewa Beach] and body boards and loves cliff jumping."

Both Jennafer and Jenna have snorkeled at Lanikai Beach on the east side of the island, and Jennafer claimed it is not the best place to snorkel. "The water can be mucky if the winds are blowing."

Jennafer and Jenna hike regularly at Koko Head Crater Trail at the Koko Head District Park and have also hiked the Maunawili Falls Trail. The Koko Head Crater Trail is popular, claimed Jennafer. "It goes straight up the mountain. You can see the east side [of Oahu] at the top; it's like stairs. A good workout."

Jenna cliff jumping at Laie Point on the
North Shore of Oahu

Jennafer said they also frequent the North Shore and especially like Waimea Bay Beach Park. "There's a large rock to jump from," which Jenna loves. They also like Spitting Cave, located on the east side of the island, which Jennafer describes as *cliff-like with rocks* that Jenna likes to jump from. "The water sucks in then shoots out." Jenna also likes China Wall, another jumping area on the east side of the island.

## SOCIALIZATION AND INTEGRATION:

Jennafer had a large support network back in Chicago, and Jenna is from a large Italian family so arriving on an island not knowing anyone was difficult for both of them. After about two weeks, Jennafer admitted they started feeling like they needed to meet some other people. They befriended a few graduate students at their initial temporary residence, but they left the island a short time after meeting them.

Jennafer started working two weeks after arrival on Oahu, but Jenna didn't start until six weeks after their arrival. Jennafer reflected on integrating into island life. "I work with a diverse group of women . . . Japanese, Filipino, Hawaiian," but claimed finding a local Hawaiian friend has helped them to integrate into the culture. Their new friend has given them insight into the history of the Hawaiian culture. "She has allowed us to ask numerous questions and kindly answered them with honesty and without judgment as we were often ignorant about the ways of living here."

Meeting neighbors resulted in some friendships. One friend is in the military and was recently transferred from Hawaii. "I miss him, but [I'm] still having lots of fun in his honor!" Jenna joked.

## HELPFUL RESOURCES:

Jennafer used Craigslist for a lot, including job and apartment hunting, and to locate several pieces of furniture she and Jenna needed. They purchased a bed at a store that delivered it to their home, and they rented a truck from Home Depot for $19 to pick up other items. Once their car arrived, they were able to put the seats down to pick up smaller items. They even borrowed their new neighbor's truck to pick up some larger items.

## LIKES:

Besides the massive number of outdoor activities available to them, Jennafer loves the weather that enables her and Jenna to enjoy

Jenna throwing shakas on a hike at Lanikai Pillboxes on the East Shore of Oahu

their active lifestyle. "We are from Chicago . . . it's 100 percent the weather," she said laughing.

One simple answer from Jenna described what she likes about Hawaii. "Everything! I love the mountains. I love the ocean. I love the atmosphere. I love the weather. I really don't think I could ever get enough of it."

"We more appreciate the free lifestyle . . . [that] we can pack up, start a new life, adjust . . . it gave us a sense of freedom and independence. We did it on our own. It showed our ability to be flexible and to acculturate," Jennafer added.

## DISLIKES:

Jennafer struggles with not being able to drive home or jump on a plane to see her family and friends. "It's hard not to go home at Christmas. Next year will make a big difference because I will make three times more money. I won't feel trapped because of finances in the future."

Besides missing her family, Jennafer craves her favorite food items the most. "I miss the chain restaurants . . . Portillo's Hot Dogs, Panera, Chipotle, Dunkin' Donuts." But the tradeoff is a lot of new foods that she and Jenna are beginning to enjoy . . . like Korean barbecue.

Jenna, in contrast, dislikes only the traffic. "I have never seen such gridlock in my life. I consider it a small price to pay to live in paradise, despite the fact that I sometimes leave my house at five a.m. to get to work by eight a.m.!"

## BEST MOMENT:

Jennafer admitted to having a lot of great moments. "Holy Cow! I'm blessed to be here. Even just driving on the North Shore . . . the different places are so beautiful."

Jenna added, "Whenever I go to the North Shore, which is probably my favorite part of the island, or especially while I'm swimming in the ocean . . . I look around me and see my surroundings, be it mountains or lush palm trees. It takes my breath away, and I realize how lucky I am to be here."

## REGRETS:

Jennafer wishes she had saved more money before relocating because it would have taken a lot of her initial anxiety away. "I solely had to rely 100 percent on Jenna. That was hard. I still want to reimburse her because that money was special to her."

Missing family is the one thing that Jenna wishes she could change. "It would be easier if flights weren't so expensive, but missing holidays and my nieces' birthdays has proven to be difficult."

## ADAPTATION:

Jennafer thinks it's easy to adapt to the Hawaiian culture because of the laidback lifestyle but also admits some difficulties. "It's hard to pronounce words . . . street names; we got lost a lot at the beginning."

Plunging into the culture on Oahu revolves around food and adventure, Jennafer admitted. She has tried the wide array of food offerings on the island, including Korean barbecue, spicy ahi, and kalua

Jenna and Jennafer seeking new experiences on a recent vacation to Kauai

(slow-cooked) pork. She and Jennafer also take full advantage of the extreme activities on the island. "We are very open-minded about new experiences."

Jennafer confessed that she measures life on Oahu two different ways: there's her life at work and her life at home. "My perspective is skewed because of the clients I work with. They don't respect me because I am young and white. Outside of work, people are very nice and polite. Our Samoan neighbors brought us food . . . but they're not engaged a lot. My co-workers are phenomenal. They introduce me to a lot." She admitted that she feels more integrated into the culture at work because her daily activities consist of meeting and talking with the long-time residents of Oahu whose families have struggled. Jenna suggested that this might be due to the loss of some Hawaiian traditions, but she is not entirely sure.

> "Other than eating a lot of sushi and trying Spam once, I really can't call myself integrated."

Jennafer said she stays positive, though, and that overall she and Jenna are adjusting well, even though it took her a while to soak in the fact that she moved so far away from her home and family.

Jenna admitted to not adapting to the Hawaiian culture at all. "Other than eating a lot of sushi and trying Spam once, I really can't call myself integrated." Though she does eat her share of Korean barbecue. "My favorite food is *poke* bowls from the Ewa Beach Foodland. I can't get enough." (*Poke* typically refers to yellowfin tuna.)

## BEST ADVICE:

Listed below is Jennafer and Jenna's advice, which gives pointers on how to make the most out of your residency in Hawaii.

- Do it! Get on the plane and go!

- ◆ Be open-minded . . . do what others suggest to experience the island fully.

- ◆ Material items are replaceable, but if permanently staying in Hawaii, take them with you.

- ◆ Find out what areas you don't want to live in before settling into long-term housing.

- ◆ Find a Hawaiian friend to help you acclimate to the island.

## VERDICT:

Jennafer would love to stay maybe one or two more years on Oahu, but she thinks it would be hard to start a practice in Hawaii without having lifelong contacts already in place to jumpstart her business.

Jenna really wants to start her career as a nurse and has to go to graduate school to do so. Therefore it depends on where she decides to attend school—in Hawaii or in Chicago. "Whatever is meant to happen will happen, [but] we will definitely go back to Chicago," Jennafer believes. We just don't know when."

> "Whatever is meant to happen will happen . . ."

Jenna is not so sure. "Do I go back home to Chicago where I would be considered a resident, pay much less, and be with my family, or do I stay where I now consider home and pay much more for the same degree? Whatever's meant to be will be."

Brittney confesses to many great moments on Kauai. "I remember the first day I came here and going to Pine Trees Beach in Hanalei, looking at the mountains and being in the ocean. . . . I knew at that moment . . . that very first day, that this is exactly where I should be."

# CASE #38691: TWO TIMES A CHARM

**Perpetrator(s):** Brittney* (34), Matthew* (30)
**Accomplice(s):** Daughter (2)
**Time In Hawaii:** 2 Years
**Island:** Kauai

## BACKGROUND:

Brittney knew she would move to Kauai after she visited the island on a vacation with her mother. What she didn't know was that she would move back and forth two times. With a history in dance, Brittney fell in love with Polynesian dancing in Texas. After performing with many groups in various events and competitions, Brittney competed in a hula competition on the Big Island. At that competition, she was invited to audition with a production company that provides authentic Polynesian entertainment. Brittney was chosen to perform with the company on the island of her choice. Acting on her connection to Kauai, she jumped at the chance to move and, within two months, she was living on the island of Kauai.

---

* *Names Have Been Changed.*

Unfortunately that stay in Kauai only lasted four years. Although Brittney found a job immediately with a property management company, the economic downturn forced Brittney into a financial crisis. She was forced to relocate back to Texas.

Brittney moved back to Texas and secured a job as a receptionist, where she met Matthew, a mechanic. It was during that whirlwind romance that Brittney wanted to give Kauai another chance. This time she had a baby on the way. "I knew I'd never leave [Texas] if I didn't do it then. If I didn't try, I'd never forgive myself," Brittney shared.

> "The year I moved back [to Texas] was the saddest time of my life. I had a good job and had a good life, but it was sad."

Once again, Brittney packed up her belongings after two years in Texas and went ahead of Matthew to Kauai. He arrived three months later but only stayed for about six months, which was just enough time to see his new baby daughter arrive. Due to some personal struggles, Matthew packed up and returned to Texas, leaving Brittney and their baby on their own for almost two years.

As a single mother on a remote island, Brittney tried to find stability but continually struggled. However, she could recall a tougher time in her life. "The year I moved back [to Texas] was the saddest time of my life. I had a good job and had a good life, but it was sad."

## FINANCES:

Brittney saved for a year to move to Kauai after she made the decision to move back to the island and, in the process, accumulated $10,000. "It wasn't a whole lot," Brittney confessed, but it helped pay the rent, deposits, and her flight with a little bit of cushion left over.

## TRAVEL AND SHIPPING:

Brittney liquidated some smaller items prior to moving, in addition to her vehicle. "My whole life that I collected is in storage," Brittney reminisced. Her larger items went into storage at her father's house, leaving her with only a few suitcases to check in at the airport.

## EMPLOYMENT:

Prior to Brittney leaving the mainland before her second move to Kauai, she secured a job at a real estate company as an agent's assistant. After beginning work for the company, she was given an ultimatum. "They weren't sympathetic to my family situation. They wanted to transfer me to the other side of the island right before Christmas."

Brittney decided to leave the company, went through seven months of unemployment, and was *barely scraping by*. After applying for a job she really wanted, she wasn't chosen, but the person who interviewed her referred her to another job that would suit her better. With no legal knowledge or experience, Brittney obtained a job working for the state in the legal department.

When Matthew arrived later, he easily obtained a job doing maintenance at a restaurant and at a shopping center. Though Brittney admits, "He's only working part-time and makes very little."

## HOUSING:

Brittney didn't experience sticker shock when it came to the housing prices. She said the rents were similar on Kauai to those in Texas.

Since Brittney had befriended some local residents during her previous time on Kauai, she had a real estate agent, who was also a friend, preview properties for her prior to her arrival. Brittney was able to secure a furnished apartment on a month-to-month rental agreement. Although the apartment was not exactly up to Brittney's standards, she said, "You don't complain over here. It doesn't get you anywhere." So Brittney quietly started searching for other housing and found a temporary option at a bed and breakfast in Wailua Homesteads, located south of Kapaa. She was able to stay there until she found more permanent housing.

> "You don't complain over here. It doesn't get you anywhere."

While searching for permanent housing, Brittney was finding properties that were unsuitable for a baby. Consequently, she decided to take the process into her own hands and place an ad on Craigslist *to see what comes to me,* she said. Her blessing came from a woman who was renting out the bottom of her *adorable* plantation home in the Kapahi area, just north of Kapaa. Brittney offered what she could afford, $1200 per month, which was much less than a three-bedroom home would rent for in that area. Her offer was accepted and soon she moved into the house.

Brittney warned that renters should not be intimidated by a month-to-month rental agreement, because they are common. Often renters will only be offered a month-to-month so the landlord can determine whether or not the tenants will be troublesome. After proving yourself, the landlord will generally agree to a longer lease term.

Matthew ended up joining Brittney again about two years after he originally left the island, and they now share an apartment in Hanamaulu with their baby. Brittney said the area where they live is low-income housing and she *hates it*. "The attitudes of the people are different [there]. They are all locals [versus tourists]; there are a lot of drugs and ice heads, and you don't want to go there with kids." She is trying to move back to Wailua Homesteads or the Kapahi area.

## SCHOOLING:

Brittney and Matthew's daughter attends an in-home day care that was recommended to them by Brittney's midwife. Although Brittney didn't have a child that needed day care on the mainland, she compared prices and found Kauai's cost of $600 per month to be similar to day care costs in Texas.

Although Brittney and Matthew's daughter is not yet in grade school, Brittney is already thinking of reserving a spot at St. Catherine's School in Kapaa because there is a one-year waiting list for admission. Brittney knows several families whose children attend St. Catherine's and the All Saints Preschool, and she has heard wonderful things about both of them. Brittney has also been warned to stay away from the public schools because they carry a *negative stigma*, but she is unsure about the specifics of this warning.

## ACTIVITIES:

Most of Brittney and Matthew's time is spent working and spending time with their daughter. Beach time is limited because of the demands of their jobs, but they do get to the beach once in a while. Brittney loves dancing hula, but the rest of their activities are simple and include *strolling through town*.

## SOCIALIZATION AND INTEGRATION:

Brittney is involved in hula on the west side of the island; through a connection with the dance group, she was invited to dance on the worship team at a church on the island.

With friends from her previous stay on Kauai, Brittney feels like a local resident. She insists, "You get what you give," on the island. Brittney agrees there is an attitude toward mainlanders, which Brittney experienced personally during her audition on the Big Island when she was confronted in the bathroom by a group of Hawaiian girls. At the time, Brittney was so *full of aloha* that she got through it and now gets along well with all of the Hawaiians. Brittney is so intertwined in the Hawaiian culture that when her friends say *those stupid haoles,* they continue with *not you, though, Brittney.*

## HELPFUL RESOURCES:

Brittney initially used Craigslist to look for housing and employment. Now she uses Craigslist when needing household supplies and furniture.

## LIKES:

Brittney has difficulty picking her favorite aspect of Kauai, but she warmly expressed, "I love the way the salt air feels on my skin when I step off the plane. I love the way drivers stop and let me in traffic and throw a shaka. I love Hawaiian music. I love the hula. I love pulling up to the credit union where I bank and seeing goats in the pasture. I love that there are chickens literally everywhere . . .

Water running in a stream down the bright red dirt of Waimea Canyon in Kauai

even leashed to the handlebars of someone's bicycle. I love that you may see a peacock crossing the road in Wailua Homesteads. I love Pidgin [talk]. I love seeing auntie sitting on the counter at the post office while reading her mail. I love the Aloha Spirit of the people. I love the land . . . the mountains, the ocean, the flowers, the red dirt. I love everything about Kauai."

## DISLIKES:

Due to Brittney's love of the island, her dislikes are nearly nonexistent. "I dislike being so far from my mom. It hurts."

## BEST MOMENT:

Brittney confesses to many great moments on Kauai. "I remember the first day I came here and going to Pine Trees Beach in Hanalei, looking at the mountains and being in the ocean. . . . I knew at that moment . . . that very first day, that this is exactly where I should be. I remember the feeling of being on stage performing at the opening of the luau I danced at and feeling the most amazing feeling. I also remember one Halloween after the show, we took a haunted train ride around the plantation and had a party in the middle of the field and danced in the rain. It was a moment I knew I would never forget. I remember watching my baby girl dance hula while she was watching me dance and my heart overflowing with happiness. I could go on and on."

## REGRETS:

Brittney and her mom are very close, but her mom is supportive of her move and visits her often. Although her mother is getting older and her daughter is growing up without being able to see her grandmother very often, Brittney remembers her connection to

Kauai. "You either love it or you don't. You know right away." And Brittney loves it. "My heart is in Hawaii."

Brittney also reflected on the year she left the island to go back to Texas. "I regret leaving for the year that I did; my heart wasn't ready to leave and it was the saddest time of my life."

## ADAPTATION:

Brittney claimed she has adapted well to Kauai. "I've made the best friends I've ever had. [They are] loving; they show up when I move my stuff. They're there for me. I didn't have that [in Texas]." She also believes part of her adaptation is linked to her Polynesian dancing, which exposed her to the Hawaiian culture.

## BEST ADVICE:

Listed below is the advice Brittney has for others. It is very simple and comes from her heart.

- Take it step by step.

- Don't ship everything right away; wait a few months to see if you want to make it permanent.

- Be humble and respectful.

- Be open-minded.

- If you're meant to be here, Kauai will open her arms and guide the way.

## VERDICT:

Brittney has no plans to return to the mainland and adamantly insists she will not leave Kauai. "Once Kauai makes it into your heart, it stays with you."

But Brittney is also sensible about her longevity on the island. "If I could, I would stay forever. This is the place I want to live and pass on . . . [but] how realistic that is with my family so far away, I don't know. I live moment for moment and keep it in God's hands."

David's first days in Hilo were noisy! "There were little frogs—coqui frogs that were super-super loud at night, kind of like crickets. There were a 1000 of them in the backyard . . . a whole jungle of frogs. It was hard to sleep the first couple nights, but it was pretty cool."

David and MacKenzie at an orchid show at Edith Kanaka'ole Stadium in Hilo

# CASE #39912: FUN STUFF

**Perpetrator(s):** David (28), MacKenzie (25)
**Accomplice(s):** 2 Cats
**Time In Hawaii:** 1 Year
**Island:** Big Island

## BACKGROUND:

Young and without commitments and responsibilities, David and MacKenzie were enjoying the activities and nightlife that Denver, Colorado, had to offer. Since MacKenzie had never lived anywhere else, she and David discussed the possibility of a move to somewhere completely different. "We wanted a big change," David said. They'd never visited Hawaii but thought it would be a complete contrast and the direct opposite of their current place of residence in Denver. On a whim, they started researching different cities on the Hawaiian Islands and found Hilo on the Big Island to be the most affordable.

Without ever visiting Hawaii, David, a construction worker, and MacKenzie, a hairdresser, decided *to do something big* and move to Hawaii. Within nine months, they were on the Big Island—only to pack up for their return to Denver one year later.

233

## FINANCES:

While David and MacKenzie's moving date was still several months away, they began saving money for their relocation. "We brought enough money to buy a car on the Big Island and to float on rent. It was at least enough to get by for one to two months," David said.

## TRAVEL AND SHIPPING:

After researching how to ship animals, David and MacKenzie decided to qualify their two cats for direct release in Hawaii, thus avoiding the quarantine process. This meant that they'd be on the mainland for another six to nine months preparing their animals for the move with the shots Hawaii required. When taking animals to Hawaii, "You have to really plan in advance," David shared.

> When taking animals to Hawaii, "You have to really plan in advance," David shared.

The animals were shipped as cargo, which David understood was a requirement on the way to Hawaii, but on the way back, there was an option to place the animals under their seats in the cabin. He recalls his feelings about directly releasing his cats to a veterinarian. "That was kind of scary considering we had to trust they would show up at the airport on time and that all the right documentation was with the cats; otherwise the airport would have held them in quarantine until everything was straightened out." Luckily that didn't happen. Overall, the total cost to ship both cats to Hawaii was about $2300, which included the shots, microchips, health certificates, rabies titer, and the plane tickets, which he recalled were around $250 each.

Prior to leaving Colorado, David sold his Volkswagen van instead of shipping it. "It didn't make sense to pay shipping costs to send an old car. I've heard stories of cars arriving [to Hawaii] messed up [with] rust damage from the time at sea." That's why he had been warned to provide covered transport for his vehicle if he shipped it. David and MacKenzie sold almost everything else that they owned, but they did ship a few boxes of clothes and smaller household items through the U.S. Postal Service. "The boxes took about a month to arrive, and the maximum weight of each box is 70 pounds with no exceptions. There were also restrictions as to the size of the box." David remembers paying about $60 to $70 per box.

David disassembled his moped and put it in two or three boxes and mailed it to himself. He intended on having it for transportation when he arrived to the Big Island, but it took too long to arrive, so he was forced to purchase a vehicle sooner than expected.

David flew to Hilo first to find housing and a job. MacKenzie and the two cats arrived two weeks later in Kona.

## EMPLOYMENT:

Immediately upon David's arrival to the Big Island, he started looking for work on Craigslist and walked around town giving out his résumé, highlighting his construction experience. "There was no work . . . no market for construction work . . . not sure why I couldn't find a job. There was no building going on there, and all the residential work was done by local handymen or as a trade or favor . . . under the radar."

David did eventually secure a job at a pizza restaurant . . . and a short time later at a car rental booth. He admitted that the jobs *weren't too bad*. He kept the car rental job until he left the island and also confessed how much fun it was to deliver pizza on his moped!

MacKenzie had her Colorado cosmetology license, and this was easy to transfer to Hawaii. Unfortunately, according to David, there was only a six-month window to transfer the license, and MacKenzie missed the deadline.

David revealed that all of the hair salons in Hilo are cheap, with haircuts costing only $10. "She was used to working in upscale salons with upscale prices." Therefore she wasn't heartbroken to avoid working in Hilo as a cosmetologist. Instead, MacKenzie secured a position at Sears in Hilo.

David and MacKenzie searched Kona for jobs, thinking the market might be better on that side of the island; however, they only found jobs in the hospitality industry and were not interested in bussing or waiting tables. Also, David wasn't fond of the desert feel of Kona.

## HOUSING:

Prior to arriving on the Big Island, David had found a room to rent in a five-bedroom house in Hilo by using Craigslist. It cost $675 per month plus $100 per month for utilities. The lady who rented the room to him picked him up at the Hilo airport. MacKenzie and the cats moved into the room with him when they arrived. A month later the couple had a *little dispute* with the owner over utility costs, so they moved out.

David and MacKenzie easily found another room to rent in a rundown plantation house near the Hilo airport. They were able to negotiate a trade agreement whereby David would provide some work on the property to prepare it for sale in exchange for a room costing $500 per month. Four months later, David and MacKenzie felt they had to leave because David claims the landlord wanted to dispose of the feral cats on the property in an inhumane manner.

David and MacKenzie then moved into a tiny studio in Hilo without a kitchen for $500 per month. They stayed there until they left the island. David shared the bright side of housing in Hilo: "No air conditioning is needed in Hilo, and only new homes have air conditioning or heat. The trade winds are good; you can just open the windows." David shared that it allowed for a lower utility cost.

David summed up his and MacKenzie's housing experience in two words: "Fun stuff!"

## SCHOOLING:

N/A

## ACTIVITIES:

David thought surfing would be fun and went a few times, but for the most part, he and MacKenzie took advantage of just going to the beach *to see the natural beauty.*

Usually they frequented Hilo Bay Beachfront Park, which David claimed didn't have any sea life or reefs. They also spent time at Richardson Ocean Park in Hilo where David said, "There is good snorkeling, lava rock, and lots of fish."

Snorkeling wasn't one of David's favorite activities

David visiting Waipio Valley

though. "MacKenzie snorkeled a lot," but David admitted, "I'm scared of the water. I tried but I couldn't breathe." Although it was difficult for him, he did try snorkeling and was amazed. "We loved seeing the sea turtles which are huge . . . three to four feet across."

David and MacKenzie also hiked a lot and tried to experience as many trails as they could. One of their favorite trails was Pu'u 'O'o Trail, and David said, "It was a great 10-mile hike." He also recalled another great hike. "The Crater Rim Trail just reminded me of what I imagined [in] some prehistoric landscape, where a dinosaur might come walking out at any minute."

## SOCIALIZATION AND INTEGRATION:

David befriended others at the pizza restaurant where he initially worked. He tried to meet people at bars but revealed, "It's usually a pretty limited scene." He shared that most socializing is done on the front porch. "It's hard to socialize with locals unless it's through others or you work with them. They keep to themselves." David admitted he hasn't experienced any hostility but has felt some racial discrimination from Hawaiians. "Most don't care for white people. It could be excused as cultural things, but I knew the truth."

## HELPFUL RESOURCES:

Although David found his car on Craigslist, he admitted, "I really did not use it that heavily. We didn't need much. We lived light." He also found that most of the Craigslist items were in Kona and this was *too long of a drive for a coffee table*. David also didn't want to start purchasing items until he and MacKenzie found a place to live that they liked; however that didn't happen. "We were able to shop at the stores in Hilo for the few things we needed."

## LIKES:

David loved the tropical environment of Hilo. "There's a lot of natural life . . . more plants . . . greener than in Denver." But he claimed this was a two-sided coin. "I liked the pace of living, slow and mellow. No one is in a hurry. People are overly nice in traffic and on the road." However, he admitted that that can also be annoying at times.

David also enjoyed being near an active volcano. "It's pretty cool . . . certain things that were never part of daily life like an earthquake tremor and a tsunami warning. People are worried about atomic dust." Although David likes living close to the volcano, it also has a downside. "The vog was a concern. There are health risks . . . the local weather gives vog ratings as part of the weather report." This was something he had never seen before. But it turned out, David said, that the vog was only a problem on the Kona side and south side of the island because of the trade winds.

There was a lot of wildlife David and MacKenzie were surprised to see. "The mongoose were really cool to see,

Grey the Stray at David and MacKenzie's shack in Hilo

and unexpected, too. There were a great deal of rats, which I also thought were cute, like really large field mice. The bugs were massive there, too. There was this huge roach that lived under the floorboards somewhere that came out periodically over the course of a few months. Half the time it didn't really even bother to run away so we ended up giving it a name . . . Beatrice."

After David and MacKenzie visited the Kona area, he realized that he liked Hilo much more. "Kona is not nearly as beautiful as Hilo."

## DISLIKES:

David reiterated his aggravation with the slowness in Hawaii, which was especially annoying when he needed to get something done in a certain amount of time.

Although David loved the tropical nature of the Hilo area and the plentiful housing, he said it was tough to find a decent job. He felt very lucky to get the two jobs he had but shared that there was a lack of opportunity on the island. "Safeway opened in Hilo. It was the biggest job opportunity available; there were 700 applicants per position." He applied but never received a call to go for an interview.

## BEST MOMENT:

When David arrived in Hilo, he stepped back and considered his new home carefully. "The first couple days I was overwhelmed and concerned mostly about getting a job. It was a little bit surreal. It was super green, there were little frogs—coqui frogs that were super-super loud at night, kind of like crickets. There were a 1000 of them in the backyard . . . a whole jungle of frogs. It was hard to sleep the first couple nights, but it was pretty cool." David researched the noise he heard and found, interestingly, that the frogs are not indigenous to Hawaii and came from Costa Rica in the early 90s.

## REGRETS:

Knowing what I know now, I wouldn't go [back] because of what the state puts cats through. [Besides that], I would go through everything else again," David shared. He also wouldn't ship anything or would ship the few items he did a little earlier.

## ADAPTATION:

David admits to *adapting but not integrating.* Immediately upon arriving to the Big Island, he changed his phone number to a phone number with the Hawaii 808 area code so he could be called back for a job. He obtained a Hawaii driver's license, which he claims may have helped him avoid being hassled at a police checkpoint. David even recognized that he picked up the Hawaiian accent. These things contributed to him being perceived as a local resident.

David claimed, "By outward appearances of Hawaiians . . . people think *lovely Hawaiians.* They welcome you, but they won't share their culture, but they're nice. They [just] don't let you into their personal space."

## BEST ADVICE:

Although David thinks if you want to relocate to Hawaii, *you should go for it!* He offered some helpful tips, listed below, that will help to avoid surprises.

- Everyone's experience is different; don't expect the same experience.

- There's a loose way of doing business.

- If you have pets, they will have to go through a lot to relocate.

- Hawaii feels like an English-speaking foreign country.

- You will find a cheap place to live on the Big Island.

## VERDICT:

David and MacKenzie would consider going to Hawaii again, but only on vacation. They would never consider living there again, even though *it's a beautiful place.*

Driving the road to Hana is one of Danielle's favorite activities. "The scenery is so beautiful—it doesn't compare to anything."

Danielle enjoying the water near Lahaina

# CASE #32199: FROM HEARTBROKEN TO HEALED

**Perpetrator(s):** Danielle (24)
**Accomplice(s):** None
**Time In Hawaii:** 5 Months
**Island:** Maui

## BACKGROUND:

Pursuing a Bachelor of Arts degree in political science in Pueblo, Colorado, and only one month away from graduation, Danielle contemplated the next phase of her life, one being the possibility of continuing on to law school. It wasn't until the day her boyfriend broke her heart that she had some clarity. She spontaneously called her dad, a Maui resident, whom she had previously visited. "I'm ready to move."

Danielle's dad was supportive, but most others thought she was crazy. "It was a blind decision. I had no responsibility. It was a good time to wallow in my heartbreak and a good time to reconnect with my dad."

Just one month later, Danielle landed on the island of Maui after her dad purchased an airline ticket for her. Unfortunately, her stay

243

in Maui ended abruptly; she hurried back to Colorado just five short months later to help her mother recover from a medical difficulty.

## FINANCES:

Working as a server throughout college, Danielle hadn't stockpiled a significant amount of money, but she had enough for her first month's rent on Maui. After her father purchased her airline ticket, Danielle only had to worry about a job and housing. Fortunately, he helped her with that as well. Her dad helped her secure a job and put a deposit down on an apartment in the same complex where he lived. "My dad was my saving grace."

## TRAVEL AND SHIPPING:

Danielle lived with her mother while she was in college, so packing up for Maui was easy. "I took two suitcases and a carry-on with clothes and other necessities." She left her vehicle and other belongings with her mother. "It's too expensive to ship vehicles. It's more cost effective to buy a car on Maui. Cars that no one wants to drive on the mainland are all people drive in Hawaii."

Danielle planned on riding the bus upon arrival to Maui and shared, "Taking the city bus is amazing! Even now in Pueblo . . . I see a bus go by and I can't imagine using it, but in Hawaii tons of people use it." Danielle maintained that it's normal to ride the bus and to hitchhike. "It's just hard trying to get home from work when the bus stops at seven or eight p.m."

## EMPLOYMENT:

Danielle applied for restaurant jobs online prior to leaving Pueblo. Thankfully, shortly after she started looking, her dad was able to secure her a serving position at the restaurant where he worked in

The sunset from Danielle's place of employment in Lahaina

Lahaina, which is frequented by tourists more than by locals. "That was the biggest thing for me," Danielle confessed. "I started the job two days after I arrived." That is not when Danielle wanted to start. "I was nervous about reintroducing myself. I wanted to be a tourist for a while first." As a self-described introvert, starting a job with strangers so quickly was out of Danielle's comfort zone.

A month after starting her serving position in Lahaina, Danielle began looking for another job. "I got another restaurant job at more of a local spot [where] islanders go, not tourists. It's a totally different experience [serving locals] than tourists. It was definitely more laidback inside. It was a very homey, fun atmosphere." Danielle worked at one of her jobs in the morning and the other at night.

"They were on the same street. After one job, I just walked down the street to the next one."

Danielle said she learned quickly in Hawaii that it's very easy to get a job in a restaurant. "You make good money. There are definite slow seasons in Maui—[but] if you live conservatively, as most people do, it's not difficult [to get by]."

## HOUSING:

On Danielle's first night in Hawaii, she stayed with her father in his studio apartment in Honokowai on the west side of Maui. The next day, she received the keys to her apartment, which was in the same complex as her father's apartment. For $1200 per month, Danielle had an unfurnished studio that included utilities.

Danielle's decision to leave her belongings at home didn't bother her. "So many people come and go on Maui . . . shops sell furniture cheap . . . hotels sell old furniture really cheap." Her dad provided her with a full-size mattress, and she purchased a bedroom set for only $269 at Paradise Living, a used furniture store in Lahaina.

Danielle calls Honokowai ". . . an amazing spot to be in. Not too far from hotels and Kaanapali beaches. The apartments are right across the street from a beach park—[and] the bus picks up in front of the apartments."

The little studio apartment in Honokowai was Danielle's home for the five months that she spent on Maui.

## SCHOOLING:

Danielle's thoughts of law school still lingered while in Hawaii. She registered and paid $100 online (http://www.lsac.org/) for the Law School Admission Test and then traveled to Oahu one weekend to take the exam that all the law schools require. To keep herself busy and to build her résumé, she enrolled in an online certification program to teach English as a Second Language.

The only thing Danielle knew for sure was that she didn't want to continue working boring part-time jobs that she was not passionate about.

## ACTIVITIES:

Danielle's favorite activity *by far* is surfing. "It's amazing and scary at the same time. It's intimidating to realize what's under that little board." According to Danielle, there's a good spot for beginning surfers in front of the town of Lahaina. "That's where classes go with beginners." Danielle also explained that there are good beaches for surfing about 10 minutes south of Lahaina town where there is good sand. "No one pulls off there. Tourists don't need to stick to the resort beaches." Danielle does warn others that some of the hidden surfing spots have surfing packs (groups of local surfers). "They will be mean and tear up your car."

Driving the road to Hana is one of Danielle's favorite activities. "The scenery is so beautiful—it doesn't compare to anything."

Danielle visiting Pearl Harbor on Oahu

## SOCIALIZATION AND INTEGRATION:

Danielle did admit that when vacationing on Maui with her boyfriend, she did encounter aggression by residents. "Locals are not open to white people." She recalled once a bus passing her and little kids yelling out the window, *"Haoles!"* Danielle insisted that if you stay long enough on the island, get a little tan, and work where the locals are, they're nice and open and friendly. "There's hope."

Without a car, Danielle had a tougher time meeting people and being flexible. She met most people at work, who she said were *cool people with cool stories.* She had fun sharing relocation stories with others.

Danielle also met others on the bus. "Everyone is so much more friendly [on Maui than on the mainland]. It's normal to exchange numbers on the bus and to meet up later." She revealed that she could probably have met others more easily if she hadn't chosen to be closed off to them because of her heartbreak. Thankfully, Danielle was widely accepted by the many people her father knew. It also helped that he was well liked!

## HELPFUL RESOURCES:

Danielle found everything she needed on the island and found enough small shops and a Walmart for things she needed, but it was more expensive than on the mainland. "It's hard to get used to at first," Danielle reflected regarding the cost of goods in Hawaii.

The single most helpful resource Danielle found on Maui is other people. "There's a lot of stuff locals will know. Ask questions; it helps to break down the barriers."

## LIKES:

Danielle likes the culture of Maui where people don't seem to focus on material goods. "I love that people [in Hawaii] have different priorities and are so different. Some people don't spend money on an apartment or car and they shower at public beaches. They live on the beach."

Danielle recalled that her dad once pointed out *attractive people who were dressed nice,* but shockingly, she learned, they were also homeless! Her curiosity led her to question *Why?* Her dad responded, "They just live on the beach. It's normal out here." Danielle maintained that she could never live like that, but she admitted, "I can see how, to some people, that's living the dream." She likes that the passions of many people living on Maui are more about the land, nature, and the outdoors. "So many people lose that [on the mainland]."

Danielle maintained that Maui has helped her set her priorities right. "It's hard to be self-conscious or [to] have any worries. I fell in love with [Maui]."

## DISLIKES:

After a while, Danielle said the size of Maui started to bother her. "I yearned to drive for an hour in one direction without turning around."

Danielle admitted she would also worry about the storms if she lived on Maui long term. "There was one huge tropical storm warning, but it ended up nothing. It was very intimidating. There aren't many options if it's bad. There's only so much higher ground."

## BEST MOMENT:

The best moments on Maui for Danielle were internal. "At first I was so heartbroken . . . after a couple weeks and still feeling pain in a place so beautiful where others are so happy. It's hard to look back at Hawaii." She sometimes wishes she had cherished the experience more with the land and people. "I felt like a silent observer. I tried to find where people found their happiness. It kept coming back to their passions about art and nature that we don't make time for [on the mainland]."

## REGRETS:

Both Danielle's arrival on and departure from Maui went smoothly, thanks to her father's help. When he purchased her original plane ticket to Maui, he purchased it as a round-trip ticket. Although he didn't expect Danielle to leave so soon; he thought she could use the ticket to visit the mainland.

The biggest regret Danielle had was that she didn't take more pictures and videos of her experiences. "I had hundreds and hundreds of pictures and videos of scenery but no pictures of people or experiences." Near the end of Danielle's stay on the island, however, she did start to take more pictures of her and her dad.

## ADAPTATION:

Because Danielle kept to herself during her time on Maui, the changes she experienced were personal. "It made such an impact on my life. I learned *Why waste time getting ready . . . Why try to look perfect?*" She found new self-confidence and completely changed her passions in life. "I am now starting school for metaphysical science." This is all because of her experiences on Maui.

## BEST ADVICE:

After reflecting on her moving experience, Danielle offered some advice, listed below, for others who want to move to Hawaii.

- ◆ Hands down, do it!

- ◆ If you are open to living with others, it's easy to find roommates, which will help to keep costs down.

- ◆ Restaurant jobs are a good place to start; they're easy to find.

- ◆ Use the bus! You meet people and you overhear things that will help you.

- ◆ Sell your belongings; there's an abundance of furniture to buy on the island.

## VERDICT:

Danielle admitted that she would love to move back to Maui, but only if she had some things in place. "I need to be financially stable to get everything I want out of the island; it sucks—but you definitely need money. There's no upward movement; it's hard to progress business-wise."

Danielle also has a dream of what her life would look like if she could save money prior to relocating again. "I need a vehicle to explore the hidden parts of the island. My dream would be a Hawaiian dream . . . having my own house, a garden, and land to sustain myself, like in Paia, a plantation town. I want to feel at home."

Patrick described a bite from a centipede as ". . . getting shot with a red hot needle filled with acid!"

Patrick and his daughter Tory (see story on Tory)

# CASE #39851: LOVE AT FIRST SIGHT

**Perpetrator(s):** Patrick (64)
**Accomplice(s):** Chihuahua
**Time In Hawaii:** 10 Years
**Island:** Molokai

## BACKGROUND:

Visiting the Hawaiian Islands as far back as the 1970s, Patrick's fondness for the islands started when he was young. Hopping aboard a sailboat at 23 years old that he purchased with his cousin, he endured a 25-day trip amidst the turbulent Pacific waters. After landing on the Big Island where he spent several months, he continued on to Maui where he stayed for two months, then moved on to his final destination, the island of Lanai. Patrick remembered, "[I] spent the better part of 1974 living on the boat in a slip at Manele Harbor." Recalling his stay on Lanai, Patrick remembered fondly that his life involved almost daily kayaking trips to Maui just for ice cream. "It was a big adventure," he said, but promised himself he'd never do that again. However, he later sailed from Martha's Vineyard to the Bahamas.

Before he relocated to Molokai, Patrick lived in Tucson, Arizona. He often traveled to faraway places, including all of the major Hawaiian Islands except for Molokai. After reading a book that described an island that was *reminiscent of yesteryear*, Patrick decided the small island of Molokai was worth checking out.

Reserving a month-to-month vacation rental on Molokai, Patrick intended on a six-month stay, ". . . long enough to see if I liked it and if anybody liked me." One week in, he placed an offer on a house and made himself a permanent resident of Molokai.

## FINANCES:

Patrick had already planned on moving from his hometown once he retired from his career in the messenger service industry, so there was no last-minute financial planning. Once he purchased his home on Molokai, he didn't have to scramble to figure out how to pay for his existence on the remote island.

## TRAVEL AND SHIPPING:

Since Patrick was already vacationing on Molokai when he purchased his house, the few bags of luggage he'd packed held all he had for a while. After he closed on his new Molokai home, he went back to Tucson and filled two lift vans, crates specifically designed for international shipping.

After Patrick sent the crates off to Hawaii, he drove his vehicle to Long Beach, California, and shipped it separately inside a crate through Matson (http://www.matson.com/).

Two years after Patrick moved to Molokai, his daughter moved to Oahu (see story on Tory). To help her out, he went back to Tucson, her hometown too, and packed and shipped five more lift vans through Matson, which included all of her belongings. Since the larger ships only travel to the major islands, Tory's crates were dropped off on Oahu while Patrick's continued on to Molokai through Young Brothers, Limited, an inter-island shipping service.

Though it's been 10 years since Patrick relocated to Molokai, he remembers the difficulty of shipping his dog, a Chihuahua. "It's a timing issue . . . a puzzle . . . not for the faint-hearted." Back then, Patrick claimed that animals were not allowed to fly in the cabin under the seat so his dog had to fly in cargo. "It was the second year after direct release [of animals started]. It took six months [to get the dog ready to fly]."

## EMPLOYMENT:

Since Patrick was retired when he relocated to Molokai, he didn't need to work. However, seven years into his residency, he picked up some handyman jobs for something to do.

## HOUSING:

When Patrick lived on Lanai back in his 20s, he lived on his sailboat in the harbor. A year after that sailboat trip to Hawaii, he purchased a home on the Big Island in Waipio Valley, and he had owned it for 15 years. About 12 years after the sale of that Big Island house and after a week of vacationing on the island of Molokai, he purchased a house for $140,000 on the drier side of the island close to the town of Kaunakakai. Patrick said playfully, "There are home loans available on the small island. The average house price is $600,000." He was thankful he was able to purchase a house for such a low price. "There were only six houses in my price range for sale!"

When Patrick compared owning a home on Molokai to owning one in Arizona, he revealed that his house on Molokai is made of redwood and is resistant to termites, unlike most homes in southern Arizona. Though he claimed it doesn't need to be treated for termites, he admitted that he did, indeed, tent the house upon purchase just to make sure.

The mold issue is not an issue in Patrick's house, he reported. "I sponge out the shower after every use." This helps to keep the mold away.

Though Patrick has a window air conditioning unit, he only uses it occasionally. His electric bill is around $150 per month, which he claims is low considering that Molokai's cost per kilowatt hour is four times the national average.

## SCHOOLING:

N/A

## ACTIVITIES:

Patrick doesn't kayak as much as he used to when he first moved to Molokai, but he and his daughter recently kayaked the Napali Coast on Kauai with a tour group. Though he doesn't visit the other islands often anymore, he and his daughter took a bicycle coasting tour to Haleakala National Park on Maui. "The tour van takes you up to a parking lot at the crater's edge before sunrise. We and many others watched the sunrise over Haleakala and then coasted down to the town of Paia."

Patrick with his daughter visiting Haleakala on Maui

Patrick likes to make a *long after-noon* of shelling where he finds Puka shells that are bead-like and popular in Hawaiian jewelry making. "I have made five or six chokers for women I've liked, but actually I like picking [out the shells] more. It is a form of therapy for me . . . and a five-mile hike."

"Fishing isn't as good as it used to be," Patrick confessed. He claims the water is either all fished out or there aren't as many fishermen anymore . . . or both. "I used to like fishing as much as sex. In the Florida Keys, it was way better than in Hawaii. It's hard to believe."

## SOCIALIZATION AND INTEGRATION:

Patrick admits he is an amateur astronomer. He has several large telescopes that he uses to host star parties to view the night sky. He does shows for schools, churches, and other youth programs. "It has given me access to everyone on the island." This has helped Patrick to integrate more with others on the island.

## HELPFUL RESOURCES:

Patrick orders from Amazon when needed items are not within reach on Molokai. When he visits his daughter on Oahu, he always shops at Home Depot and Costco. When he needs larger items, Patrick purchases them from a store that has all used items from the hotels. "My refrigerator was freight damaged. The stove is used from a military base."

## LIKES:

The list of Patrick's likes was easy: "Number one, the weather. You can do what you want when you want." Though he doesn't take advantage of the beach and the water much, ". . . I just enjoy looking at it and seeing the guys surf." Patrick also likes how clear the air is, but sometimes the vog from the Big Island affects Molokai. (See Dislikes.)

The small-town feel of Molokai was the initial draw for Patrick, but getting used to the lack of amenities took some time.

"There is no fast food. It's a real small main street . . . three or four blocks long. The whole town is like a neighborhood with two gas stations . . . no stoplights. And the police are lenient; there is virtually no crime."

Patrick loves that his daughter Tory is close by on Oahu. "My options were open. I could have moved anywhere. I thought of Mexico, Europe, and Australia; my aunt and cousin are the only ones left besides Tory. I thought mostly [of] where she could visit easily. She was a big factor of moving to Hawaii."

## DISLIKES:

According to Patrick, the vog is of major concern to the islands and significantly affects Molokai for about 30 days a year. "It kills crops on Maui. People move because of respiratory problems." He even had an eye issue in which vog may have been the primary factor. "There are days on Oahu that look like L.A. smog!"

Though Patrick thinks the variety of people on Molokai makes it interesting, he said there is quite a bit of racism. "There are Japanese, Filipino, Portuguese, Chinese, Puerto Rican—a good mix of people." However, he claimed that even those who are not Hawaiian have a superior attitude toward newcomers.

> According to Patrick, the vog is of major concern to the islands and significantly affects Molokai for about 30 days a year.

The variety of food on the island is scarce, Patrick said. "There are 12 restaurants and 10 of them serve Filipino food." This forces Patrick to cook more often. "Fish is available but it's rare and expensive. You'd be surprised. During Chinese New Year, the Red Fish, Onaga, is over $30 per pound. It's normally $7–12 per pound." He often goes to the harbor and buys fish from the only fisherman left on Molokai. "He gives me the worst one, like the one that's missing an eye!" The fisherman sends the rest to Oahu.

Patrick expressed plenty of centipede grievances! He recounted how he has been bitten six or seven times in his 10-year residency on Molokai. One night around 3:00 a.m. he was bitten on his calf by a centipede. He woke up, rolled over, and the centipede had crawled under him and bit him on the back. "It's like getting shot with a red hot needle filled with acid," Patrick remembered vividly. The centipede continued to climb quickly over his chest toward his face. Patrick finally was able to flick it off onto the floor, but it was so quick it got away. It was about six inches long.

> "Centipedes are the worst thing by far. If I move, I will be glad to be away from those god damn centipedes!"

The centipede bites don't end with that bedtime story. Since centipedes tend to gravitate to moist, warm areas, three or four friends of Patrick's have been stung on their testicles. "They're demonic," insisted Patrick. "You can cut them in half and put the two halves in a jar, and they will fight to the death."

Another night that Patrick calls *The Night of the Centipedes*, he killed three in the house and one on the porch. Another time he was taking a shower and one came up through the drainpipe. "It climbed up my leg to my thigh . . . [and] it barely stung me," before he was able to knock it away.

To top it off, there is no way to avoid the centipedes, Patrick said. "Maybe on Oahu in a top floor condo, but a second floor or third floor . . . you can't avoid them." He maintained, "Centipedes are the worst thing by far. If I move, I will be glad to be away from those god damn centipedes!"

## BEST MOMENT:

When Patrick arrived to Molokai, he fell in love with the island in the first week and knew he wanted to be there. He felt like he'd moved back in time to the 1950s. "I lock my door now, but I didn't used to for years. There's a safe feeling . . . no gangs, murders, muggings. You know damn near everybody."

Patrick and Tory during his early days in Hawaii

## REGRETS:

"If I [had] moved to the Big Island, I would have had regrets because of the vog. Kona made a jump of a little fishing village to a ridiculous tourist trap." But Patrick has had no regrets about moving to Molokai.

## ADAPTATION:

When Patrick first moved to Molokai, he believed he was fairly well accepted by Hawaiians and others alike but not completely accepted by either. "There are locals and haoles. There are always issues." He reflected on the attitudes of the people. "Hawaiians are like kids; they can be dangerous and provoked but would rather not have a confrontation."

Patrick also claimed the non-Hawaiians display superior attitudes. "Somehow they think if they were here first, you should bow down to them." But that doesn't bother Patrick. "It's more prevalent on Maui. Molokai is one of the nicer spots."

Patrick maintained that he has adapted to the Hawaiian way of life. "It's a very interesting place in a foreign way."

## BEST ADVICE:

Patrick only offers a benefit of living in Hawaii. "Your health will be better, and you will live longer [in Hawaii]." However, he does warn to be prepared for centipedes!

## VERDICT:

Patrick pondered the thought of leaving Hawaii. "I could move someday. I might . . . without being torn apart. Maybe Bisbee [Arizona]. It's cheap, and it has good weather."

**Will Hawaii be your next address?**

# GLOSSARY

**Aina (EYE-na):** Earth or land

**Aloha (ah-LO-ha):** In the Hawaiian language means hello, good-bye, or a feeling of affection, peace, compassion, and mercy

**Aloha Spirit:** Treating people with deep care and respect

**Auntie:** A beautiful way to show respect when addressing or referring to elder females

**Beachcombing:** Searching a beach looking for things of value

**Haole (HOW-leh):** Originally meaning a foreigner; now meaning a Caucasian or one who is not native to Hawaii

**Hawaiian:** This term is used in this book to describe a descendant of Hawaiian ancestry, not one who resides in the state of Hawaii

**Honu (HO-noo):** Hawaiian Green Sea Turtle

**Kava (KAH-vah):** A narcotic sedative drink made in Polynesia from the crushed roots of a plant of the pepper family

**Kuleana (Koo-lee-AH-na):** Right, privilege, and responsibility

**Lanai (LA-NIGH):** Porch or patio

**Leeward:** Western side of the island

**Mainland:** The continental United States (48 contiguous states)

**Off-Grid:** Not being connected to a main power or water source

**Ohana (oh-HA-na):** Family, but often used as a term for a guest house

**Pidgin:** Hawaii's Creole language

**Shaka (SHA-ka):** Sometimes known as hang loose, a hand gesture often associated with Hawaii and surf culture

**Vog:** A form of air pollution that results from gases emitting from an erupting volcano.

**Windward:** Eastern side of the island

# ACKNOWLEDGMENTS

First and foremost, I thank the Lord Jesus for giving me the fortitude to propel forward and allow me to spend my life writing if I so choose.

Without the gracious time and energy of those who have shared their intimate stories within these pages, this book would not have been possible. Thank you for opening your life to me and to the rest of the world.

I thank my husband who supports my dreams and works hard so I can stay home and do as I please.

I thank my children who have sacrificed time with me while I locked myself in my office for hours and hours interviewing and writing.

Thanks to my mom for showing an interest in my writing and for encouraging me to use my skills.

I also thank my dad who passed away two years ago. He was always my fan and would be proud of me.